W9-CEV-596

ENDANGERED ANIMALS OF
AFRICA

WORLD
BOOK

a Scott Fetzer company
Chicago
worldbook.com

Staff

Executive Committee

President
Donald D. Keller
Vice President and Editor in Chief
Paul A. Kobasa
Vice President, Sales
Sean Lockwood
Vice President, Finance
Anthony Doyle
Director, Marketing
Nicholas A. Fryer
Director, Human Resources
Bev Ecker

Editorial

Associate Director,
Annuals and Topical Reference
Scott Thomas
Managing Editor,
Annuals and Topical Reference
Barbara A. Mayes
Senior Editor,
Annuals and Topical Reference
Christine Sullivan
Manager, Indexing Services
David Pofelski
Administrative Assistant
Ethel Matthews
Manager, Contracts & Compliance
(Rights & Permissions)
Loranne K. Shields

Editorial Administration

Senior Manager, Publishing
Operations
Timothy Falk

Manufacturing/ Production

Director
Carma Fazio
Manufacturing Manager
Sandra Johnson
Production/Technology
Manager
Anne Fritzinger
Proofreader
Nathalie Strassheim

Graphics and Design

Art Director
Tom Evans
Senior Designer
Don Di Sante
Media Researcher
Jeff Heimsath
Manager, Cartographic Services
Wayne K. Pichler
Senior Cartographer
John M. Rejba

Marketing

Marketing Specialists
Alannah Sharry
Annie Suhy
Digital Marketing Specialists
Iris Liu
Nudrat Zoha

Writer

A. J. Smuskiewicz

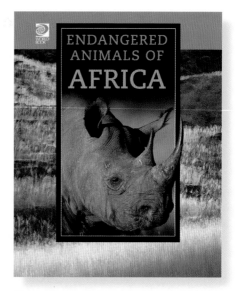

The cover image is the endangered black rhinoceros.

World Book, Inc.
233 North Michigan Avenue
Chicago, Illinois 60601 U.S.A.

For information about other World Book publications, visit our website at **www.worldbook.com** or call **1-800-WORLDBK (967-5325).**
For information about sales to schools and libraries, call 1-800-975-3250 (United States) or 1-800-837-5365 (Canada).

Library of Congress Cataloging-in-Publication Data

Endangered animals of Africa.
    pages cm. -- (Endangered animals of the world)
  Summary: "Information about some of the more important and interesting endangered animals of Africa, including the animal's common name, scientific name, and conservation status; also includes a map showing the range of each animal featured; and a glossary, additional resources, and an index"--Provided by publisher.
  Includes index.
  ISBN 978-0-7166-5621-0
  1. Endangered species--Africa--Juvenile literature. 2. Rare animals--Africa--Juvenile literature. 3. Animals--Effect of human beings on--Africa--Juvenile literature. I. World Book, Inc.
  QL83.E527 2015
  591.68096--dc23
                                   2014019653

Endangered Animals of the World
ISBN: 978-0-7166-5620-3 (set)

Printed in China by Shenzhen Donnelley Printing Co., Ltd. Guangdong Province
1st printing October 2014

Contents

Why species in Africa are threatened

Africa has an astonishing variety of wildlife. Thousands of different kinds of mammals, reptiles, amphibians, fish, birds, and insects live in its forests, deserts, and grasslands. Unfortunately, this massive continent has many fewer wild animals than it did even 100 years ago. And the animal *species* (types) that live there are not as widespread as they once were.

Some 2,800 species in Africa are threatened, many critically. Of course, this number includes only those known to science. Many species remain undiscovered. And almost certainly, a number of these animals are in peril or have even disappeared.

Gradual shifts in climate over thousands of years account for some of the problems affecting Africa's wildlife. But in many areas, human activities are the main reason for the animals' decline.

Threats. A loss of *habitat* may be the greatest threat to African wildlife. (A habitat is the kind of place in which an organism usually lives.) Ancient forests, particularly rain forests, have been cut down for their wood and to make room for human settlements. Grasslands have been converted into pasture for livestock. Marshlands have been drained for farmland. Most species are specially adapted to live and reproduce in a specific habitat and cannot survive when this habitat is destroyed.

Africa's wild animals have often been hunted—sometimes overhunted—for pleasure or captured for pets, zoos, and research laboratories. *Poachers* (illegal hunters) kill the animals for their meat and such body parts fur, tusks, horns, which are profitable on the black, or unlawful, market. Farmers and livestock owners shoot, trap, or poison animals that they view as threats to their livelihood.

Pollution from industrial, agricultural, or other sources has sickened or killed many wild animals. Diseases spread by people and such domestic animals as dogs have seriously affected some wildlife species. Chimpanzees and gorillas have died from Ebola hemorrhagic fever transmitted by humans. Both domestic and nonnative animals have preyed on or crowded out *native species* (species that occur naturally in a region).

Conservation. Conservationists face difficult challenges in protecting African wildlife. But there have been some success stories. Poaching continues to devastate elephant populations in some parts of Africa. But thanks to an international campaign, the elephant population in other places is increasing at a healthy rate.

In this volume. The species described in this volume represent the variety of endangered animals in Africa. From the smallest and simplest to the largest and most powerful, Africa's wildlife is facing challenges from its human neighbors.

Scientific sequence. The species are presented in a standard scientific sequence that generally goes from simple to complex. This sequence starts with insects or other *invertebrates* (animals without backbones) and then moves through fish, amphibians, reptiles, birds, and mammals.

Range. Red areas on maps indicate an animal's *range* (area in which it occurs naturally) on the continent of Africa.

Glossary. Italicized words, except for scientific names, appear with their definitions in the Glossary at the end of the book.

Conservation status. Each species discussed in this book is listed with its common name, scientific name, and conservation status. The conservation status tells how seriously a species is threatened. Unless noted differently, the status is according to the International Union for Conservation of Nature (IUCN), a global organization of conservation groups. The most serious IUCN status is *Extinct,* followed by *Extinct in the Wild, Critically Endangered, Endangered, Vulnerable, Near Threatened,* and *Least Concern.* Criteria used to determine these conservation statuses are included in the list to the right.

Conservation statuses

Extinct All individuals of the species have died

Extinct in the Wild The species is no longer observed in its past range

Critically Endangered The species will become extinct unless immediate conservation action is taken

Endangered The species is at high risk of becoming extinct due to a large decrease in range, population, or both

Vulnerable The species is at some risk of becoming extinct due to a moderate decrease in range, population, or both

Near Threatened The species is likely to become threatened in the future

Least Concern The species is common throughout its range

Icons. The icons indicate various threats that have made animals vulnerable to extinction.

Key to icons

 Disease

 Global warming

 Habitat disturbance

 Habitat loss

 Hunting

 Overfishing

 Pet trade

 Pollution

 Ranching

Adetomyrma venatrix

Conservation status: Critically Endangered

The frightening name of these thin-waisted, orange-colored ants comes from feeding habits that may seem gruesome to us. Dracula ants suck the blood of their own young! More precisely, hungry worker ants and *queen ants* (females that reproduce in a colony) rip and chew holes into the wormlike *larvae* (immature ants) of their colony. They then suck out the larvae's hemolymph, a special fluid in insects that is similar to blood. Although the larvae are often left with scars, most survive these vampire attacks, which has been called "nondestructive cannibalism." However, scientists have reported that the larvae try to escape when workers looking for a meal show up in the nursery. Dracula ants, of course, are named for the Transylvanian count made famous by the Irish author Bram Stoker in his 1897 novel and, since then, by numerous films.

To feed the larvae, worker ants stun other insects with *venom* (poison) delivered by long stingers. Then they drag their victims back to the colony.

Appearance. *A. venatrix* queens—unlike the queens of some Dracula ant *species* (types)—do not have wings and are yellow. Males with wings, which mate with queens, are a darker orange. Workers, which are blind, are a pale orange.

Colonies. Colonies of *A. venatrix* and other Dracula species may consist of as many as 10,000 workers as well as males with wings and several wingless queens. Some scientists have suggested that the winged males fly to other colonies to mate with queens.

New yet old. Dracula ants are relatively new to scientists. Scientists didn't know of their existence until the discovery of the species *A. venatrix* in the early 1990's. The first Dracula ant colony wasn't discovered until 2001. Since then, scientists have discovered a number of other Dracula species, including six found in 2014.

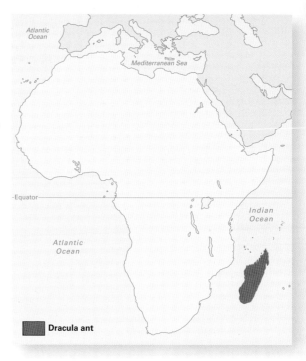

Dracula ant

Despite their recent scientific history, Dracula ants may have an ancient evolutionary lineage. Their abdomens are remarkably similar to those of wasps, from which, scientists think, ants descended about 70 million to 80 million years ago. As a result, Dracula ants may be a *missing link* (a transition species) between wasps and ants.

Habitat. Most species of Dracula ant are native to the island of Madagascar, in the Indian Ocean off the southeastern coast of Africa. They live in rotting logs and leaf litter in the island's tropical forests.

Threats. Because *A. venatrix* queens cannot fly, they must walk to new areas to start new colonies. This means they cannot travel very far and so cannot easily escape from areas in which their natural landscape is being changed by *development* (human activities affecting the natural environment). As the construction of houses, farms, businesses, dams, and roads has altered or destroyed the forest *habitat* (living place) of the Dracula ants, the ants have become seriously threatened by extinction.

The Dracula ant gets its name from its practice of sucking a bloodlike fluid from its own young.

Baboon spider

Augacephalus, Ceratogyrus, other genera

Conservation status: Protected (in South Africa)

More than 40 *species* (types) of these large, hairy spiders live in *habitats* (living places) in southern Africa, ranging from grassland to *savanna* (grassy plain) to forest. Elsewhere, baboon spiders are known as tarantulas.

Appearance. The bodies of baboon spiders, not counting their eight long legs, vary in length from about 1/2 to 3 1/2 inches (1.3 to 9 centimeters). They may be black, brown, gray, yellow, or other colors. Some types of baboon spider are named for the markings on, or the shapes of, their *carapace* (hard front segment of their body). Starburst baboon spiders—in the *genus Augacephalus*—have markings that look like rays shooting from a central point. (A genus is a group of related organisms usually made up of at least two species.) Horned baboon spiders—in the genus *Ceratogyrus*—have a hornlike structure on the top of their carapace.

Baboon spiders were so named because the last two segments of their legs resemble the finger of a baboon.

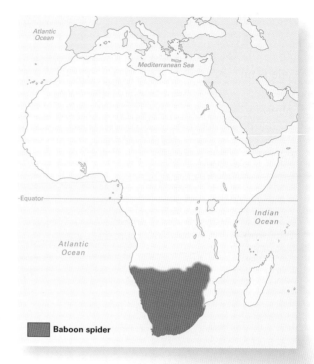

Baboon spider

As with many other kinds of spiders, female baboon spiders are larger than males. If the male is not careful when approaching the female, she may attack and eat him. Some male baboon spiders have a type of spur on their front legs that they use to force and hold open a female's fangs so she can't attack them.

Hunting. Baboon spiders hunt at night, hiding and waiting for prey. Some hide under rocks or other objects. Others dig burrows with their sharp mouthparts called chelicerae and their grasping, leglike pedipalps. The spiders line the inside of their burrow with silk that they make in special glands. The lining forms a rim at the burrow entrance. When an insect or other small animal touches the silk, vibrations warn the spider inside the burrow that prey is near. The spider then races to the entrance, pounces on the prey, and drags it into the burrow to eat.

Baboon spiders eat crickets, grasshoppers, millipedes, termites, and other small prey. The largest baboon spiders can even capture and eat small scorpions, frogs, and lizards.

Threats. Wild populations of baboon spiders—like many tarantulas elsewhere in the world—are threatened by the pet trade. Several species of baboon spiders are legally protected—meaning that it is against the law to collect, transport, or keep the spiders without a special permit. However, because of the great demand for these animals as pets, they are often captured illegally.

Rhynchobatus djiddensis

Conservation status: Vulnerable

The giant guitarfish, also called the white-spotted wedgefish, is 1 of more than 550 *species* (types) of ray, a fish that is related to the shark. The guitarfish is a fierce predator, capturing and eating such animals as fish, squid, lobsters, crabs, and clams. It does most of its hunting in shallow waters near the shore, especially in areas with coral reefs.

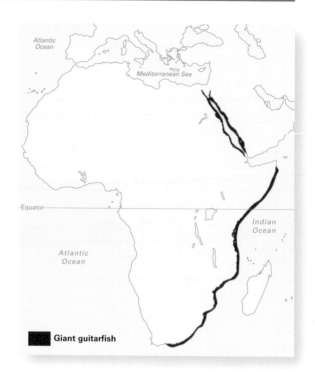

Giant guitarfish

Appearance. Like sharks, rays have a skeleton made of cartilage—a tough, elastic substance that is more flexible than bone. Unlike sharks, most rays have a flattened body with large fins behind their gill openings called pectoral fins, which resemble wings. Guitarfish have a longer, more tubular body than most other rays. If you use your imagination, you can picture the large pectoral fins of the giant guitarfish, along with its pointed snout, as the soundboard of a strange, triangular guitar. The fish's long body would be the guitar's fingerboard.

The giant guitarfish can grow to a length of about 10 feet (3 meters). But it may seem even larger when viewed from above. That's because there are two round black markings at the base of each pectoral fin that look like big, widely spaced eyes. These markings may fool a predator, such as a shark, into thinking that the guitarfish is larger than it really is—thereby protecting the guitarfish from being attacked.

Habitat. The guitarfish is most common off the eastern coast of Africa, from the Red Sea to South Africa. During winter, many guitarfish move to warmer waters closer to the equator.

Threats. Giant guitarfish populations are classified as Vulnerable because many of the fish are captured for food or sport. Their large back fins, called dorsal fins, are among the most desired type of fin used to make a popular Asian dish called shark-fin soup. The fins, which are also collected to make Asian

medicines, can fetch very high prices on the world market.

Giant guitarfish are easy to find and catch because of their large size and shallow-water *habitat* (living place). Commercial fishing ships catch them with large nets. Anglers—people who fish for sport with rods and reels—value giant guitarfish for their size and for the powerful fight that they give while being reeled in. Anglers often release guitarfish after catching them. However, scientific data suggest that many of the returned fish do not survive. Other threats to giant guitarfish come from pollution in their coastal habitats.

Adding to the giant guitarfish's vulnerability is the fact that it grows slowly. Females are not able to bear young until they are almost 6 feet (1.8 meters) long, usually at about age 7.

The guitarfish, a relative of the stingray, is often hunted for its fins, which are used to make shark-fin soup, popular in parts of Asia.

Nectophrynoides

Conservation status: Critically Endangered, Endangered, or Vulnerable

Most female frogs and toads lay gooey masses of eggs in water, where they hatch into small, fishlike tadpoles. *Viviparous* toads—also called live-bearing toads—are the only toad that does not lay eggs and whose life cycle does not include tadpoles. Rather, the females give birth to small "baby" toadlets—much like a mammal mother gives birth to mammal infants.

Appearance. Viviparous toads are typically quite small, sometimes smaller than a penny. Others are a bit larger. What they lack in size, however, they may make up for in color. Some viviparous toads sport bright shades of orange or yellow, or other bold hues. Other viviparous toads are brown or black. Individuals of the same *species* (type) may be different colors.

Habitat. There are several species of African viviparous toads, most of which live in the moist *montane* forests, grasslands, or wetlands of Tanzania, in eastern Africa. (Montane forests are forests on mountains.) During the day, the toads generally sit on leaves. They use their long, sticky tongues to capture insects or other tiny animals for food. At night, the toads hide on the ground, often under fallen trees.

Threats. The main threat to African viviparous toads is the loss of their *habitats* (living places). As the human population of Tanzania grows and spreads into natural areas, the trees and other vegetation are destroyed to make space for houses, businesses, and farms. People also cut the trees down to get wood for construction and fuel. The removal of plant life and changes to water flow disturb the toads' *ecosystems,* threatening the animals' survival. (An ecosystem consists of living organisms and their physical environment.) Collectors also pose a danger to viviparous toads.

African viviparous toad

Collectors value the amphibians because of their beautiful colors and unusual reproductive habits.

Some species of viviparous toads are critically endangered, with some on the verge of extinction. Other species of viviparous toads have relatively stable populations but remain vulnerable to ecosystem disturbances or other threats. The more stable populations are found in protected nature reserves in Tanzania.

The Kihansi spray toad (*N. asperginis*) is a yellow African viviparous toad that became extinct in its natural wetland habitat in Tanzania in 1999. The cause of its disappearance was the construction of the Kihansi hydroelectric dam. The dam nearly dried up the waterfalls that produced the misty habitat in which the toads lived.

Fortunately, some Kihansi spray toads lived in New York City's Bronx Zoo and the Toledo (Ohio) Zoo, where biologists bred them to build up the population. In 2012, many of these captive-bred toads were released into their original habitat in the Kihansi Gorge, which now has a system of sprinklers.

African viviparous toads usually spend the day sitting on leaves, catching food. They use their long tongue to capture insects and other tiny animals.

Goliath frog

Conraua goliath

Conservation status: Endangered

This *species* (type) of frog—named after the giant in the Hebrew Bible—is the largest frog in the world. It may grow to a length of 12.5 inches (32 centimeters) and a weight of more than 6.6 pounds (3 kilograms). Its big body is greenish-brown on top and yellowish-orange beneath. Its skin has a rough, grainy texture. Each of its bulging eyes is about 1 inch (2.5 centimeters) wide.

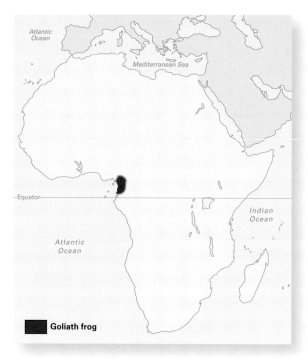

Goliath frog

Reproduction. The mating habits of the Goliath frogs are different from those of most other frogs and toads. The males of most frog species make mating calls to attract females. The male sucks air into pockets of the floor of his mouth, known as vocal sacs, and then blows the air out. But Goliath frog males do not have vocal sacs. They make their mating calls by opening their mouths to create a long, whistling sound. Females are attracted by the whistle.

The female lays a mass of hundreds of eggs on a plant at the bottom of a river or stream. She does not tend the eggs. Once the tadpoles hatch, they feed on the plant, taking about 75 to 90 days to develop into a frog with legs. Surprisingly, at hatching, the Goliath tadpole is about the same size as other tadpoles. Most of its growth takes place during its tadpole phase.

As adults, the frogs feed on insects, small fish, and shellfish. They also eat other small animals, including other frogs, newts, and salamanders. The frogs generally hunt at night.

Daily life. Goliath tadpoles spend most of their time underwater. The adults often bask on moss-covered rocks in the fast-moving streams where they live. Their greenish-brown skin provides excellent camouflage.

Habitat. Goliath frogs live in the dense tropical rain forests of Cameroon and Equatorial Guinea, on Africa's western coast. The frogs can also be found in forests near rivers.

Threats. The wild population of Goliath frogs has greatly declined for a number of reasons. Local people trap the huge frogs for food. Human settlements, commercial logging operations, and farming have claimed a significant amount of the frogs' rain forest *habitat* (living place). Other threats include pollution and the build-up of *sediment* (soil, stones, and other matter) in the streams and rivers where the frogs live and lay their eggs. The sediment comes from farming, mining, or other activities that disturb the soil. Goliath frogs prefer clean water. The frogs are also captured and exported to other countries for zoo displays, the pet trade, and even frog races.

Some Goliath frogs live in areas protected by government action, including Monte Alen National Park in Equatorial Guinea and wildlife sanctuaries in the shoreline areas of Cameroon. The government of Equatorial Guinea limits the number of Goliath frogs that can be legally exported each year. However, conservationists believe that additional steps are needed to protect these unique amphibians.

The Goliath frog is the largest frog on Earth. Most of their growth takes place during their tadpole stage.

Osteolaemus tetraspis

Conservation status: Vulnerable

Although some crocodiles can grow more than 20 feet (6 meters) long, the African dwarf crocodile, as its names indicates, is not one of those giants. In fact, it is the world's smallest crocodile *species* (type), typically reaching a length of about 5 feet (1.5 meters) and a weight of 70 pounds (32 kilograms).

Appearance. Although small (for a crocodile), the African dwarf crocodile is tough. Its thick hide—including a heavily armored back and tail—help protect it from attack by larger predators. Males are larger than females.

The crocodile's body is black to greyish-black, except for its yellowish belly, which may

African dwarf crocodile

have dark patches. Young dwarf crocodiles, which are brown and yellow, turn black as they grow older.

The dwarf crocodile has strong jaws filled with long, sharp teeth. The dwarf crocodile's alternate name—broad-nosed crocodile—describes the reptile's short, rounded snout.

Hunting. The dwarf crocodile hunts mostly at night. It searches for fish, amphibians, and such crustaceans as crabs. During the day, the crocodile usually rests in burrows with underwater entrances or among tree roots that stick out of river or pond embankments.

Estivating. In regions with severe dry seasons—when it is difficult to find water or

prey—the dwarf crocodile digs a burrow in which to *estivate*. Estivation is an inactive state that protects some animals from dryness and heat—the same way that hibernation protects other animals from cold. During estivation, the breathing, heartbeat, and other body functions slow down significantly. Estivating animals need less water and so can survive long, hot, dry periods that might otherwise prove deadly.

Reproduction. During the wet season, females build mounds of decaying plant material in which to lay their eggs. Heat released by the decay of the vegetation helps *incubate* the eggs (keep them warm enough for the baby crocodiles to grow). Typically, a female lays about 10 eggs, which hatch within 100 days.

The mother crocodile guards the nest during incubation. After the young hatch, the female carries them to the shallow edge of a river or pond, where she guards them for some weeks. Dwarf crocodiles live for about 70 years, remaining sexually active until they die.

Habitat. Dwarf crocodiles live in tropical rain forests and *savannas* (grassy plains) of west-central Africa. Their *range* extends from southern Senegal south to Angola and east to the Democratic Republic of the Congo. (Range is the area in which a certain plant or animal naturally occurs.)

Threats. Biologists believe that the main threats to African dwarf crocodiles stem from the increased pressures of human activities on their populations and *ecosystems* (living organisms and their environment). The reptiles are hunted and killed for their meat, and *deforestation* (forest destruction) is eliminating their *habitats* (living places). In addition, the hides of the dwarf crocodile are used by local people to make low-quality leather products.

The African dwarf crocodile is often hunted for its meat and its hide.

Psammobates geometricus

Conservation status: Endangered

The geometric tortoise is the rarest of three so-called "tent" tortoises in *Psammobates,* a *genus* (group of species) that lives in southern Africa. It gets its name from the complex geometric pattern of blackish-brown and yellowish markings on its high, domed shell. In 2012, the International Union for Conservation of Nature (IUCN) placed the geometric tortoise on its list of the 100 most endangered species.

Habitat. The geometric tortoise lives mainly in lowlands and valleys near the southern tip of South Africa between the mountains and the sea. It eats the unique mix of vegetation found in this area—the grasses, herbs, and shrubs of plant communities known as fynbos and renosterveld. Because of its special diet, the geometric tortoise typically does not do well in disturbed *habitats* (living places) or in captivity.

Threats. More than 90 percent of the geometric tortoise's habitat has been destroyed as a result of the development of farmland and towns. The spread of *invasive* (alien) *species*

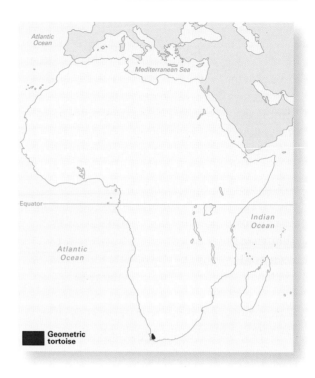

Geometric tortoise

of plants has also reduced suitable habitat. In addition, domestic dogs and pigs that have been introduced to the area prey on the tortoises and their eggs. The South African government has established some protected lands for the geometric tortoise.

The geometric tortoise has a shell with beautiful dark brown and yellow markings.

Astrochelys yniphora

Conservation status: Critically Endangered

The ploughshare tortoise is one of the rarest tortoises in the world. It is found only in northwestern Madagascar. Biologists estimate that only a few hundred of these land-dwelling individuals survive in the wild.

Shell games. This tortoise got its name because of the appearance of the lower part of its shell, which curves up between the front legs in a plough (or plow) shape. Males use this structure to try to flip over other males during wrestling matches in which they fight for females.

Reproduction. The female uses her hind legs to dig a hole in which she lays from one to six round eggs. She packs soil over the eggs and then leaves. After about 230 days, the eggs hatch. The baby tortoises—whose shells are about 1.8 inches (4.5 centimeters) long—are fully independent. The reptiles may grow more than 16 inches (40.6 centimeters) long.

Threats. The number of ploughshare tortoises has crashed for several reasons. Local people

Ploughshare tortoise

hunt them for food. *Poachers* (illegal hunters) capture them to sell as pets. Their habitat has been burned to create grazing land for cattle. Conservationists have tried to breed ploughshare tortoises in captivity to build up their numbers for release into protected areas.

The ploughshare tortoise gets its name from the piece of shell that projects from between its front legs.

Neophron percnopterus

Conservation status: Endangered

The Egyptian vulture is a striking bird with a bare, bright yellow face surrounded by a hood of white, spiky feathers. The rest of its plumage is white or pale gray, except for its flight feathers, the rigid feathers in the wing or tail, which are black. The bird is smaller than many other vultures. It averages about 27 inches (68 centimeters) in length, with a wingspan of 5.6 feet (1.7 meters).

Diet. Egyptian vultures sometimes fly 50 miles (80 kilometers) in a single day as they search for food, scanning the ground below them. However, they are not picky eaters. They eat just about anything they come across. The Egyptian vulture's diet consists mainly of dead animals, or carrion. But it will sometimes catch small live animals, including rabbits, birds, fish, and insects. And it will eat rotting fruit and vegetables, garbage, and even feces. Some people have reported seeing the birds throw stones at eggs to crack the shells and eat the contents.

Habitat. Despite its name, the Egyptian vulture has a wide *range* (area in which it naturally occurs) that extends far beyond Egypt. Some populations remain in the same area all year long. Most of those birds live in eastern Africa, the Arabian Peninsula, and India. Other populations are migratory—breeding in southern Europe and south-central Asia and wintering as far south as the Sahel region of Africa.

Egyptian vultures are usually found in open, dry *habitats* (living places), including deserts and *steppe* grasslands (level, treeless plains). They typically build their nests in such rocky places as ledges, cliffs, or caves. Their nests are sometimes found in tall trees. Both males and females construct the large nests out of sticks, hair, rags, and other materials. Both parents also work together to *incubate* the eggs (keep them warm) and feed the chicks.

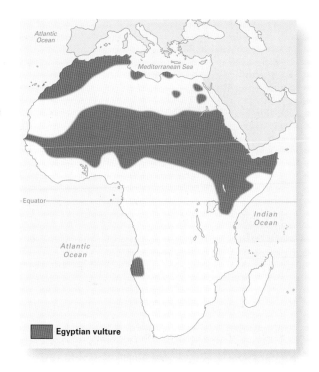

Egyptian vulture

Threats. The Egyptian vulture is endangered for many reasons. The bird's population in India was devastated by poisoning from a drug that was used to promote the health of livestock. The vultures took in the drug when they fed on livestock carcasses. In Africa, overgrazing by livestock has disturbed the bird's habitat. In addition, the decline in the populations of wild hoofed animals reduced the bird's carrion supply. In Europe, many vultures have been poisoned by lead from gun ammunition and electrocuted by power lines. The bird's food supply was reduced by government regulations controlling the disposal of animal carcasses.

Actions to protect the Egyptian vulture include the establishment of protected reserves, the banning of the harmful livestock drug, and the relaxation of laws on the disposal of animal carcasses.

The Egyptian vulture, which was sacred to the ancient Egyptians, was known as "pharaoh's chicken" because it was so common.

Geronticus eremita

Conservation status: Critically Endangered

The northern bald ibis has been listed as one of the 100 most endangered animals in the world by the IUCN. The ibis's population in the wild has crashed since the mid-1900's, though several thousand of the birds survive in zoos.

Appearance. The northern bald ibis has a unique appearance. Its head is mostly naked, but the rest of its body is covered with long, dark feathers that have a glossy, bluish-purple sheen. Its beak is long, curved, and reddish.

Diet. Northern bald ibises forage for a wide variety of foods. They look for insects, spiders, scorpions, worms, snails, and other small animals, using their long beak to probe into rock cracks and to peck at the ground. They sometimes capture such larger animals as fish and mice. They will even eat dead animals—a seemingly appropriate diet for this vulturelike bird. The ibises will also feed on such plant foods as berries and duckweed.

Breeding. During the breeding season, the birds nest in colonies of about 40 individuals, usually on mountain cliffs or rocky slopes. They build their nests from tree branches and then line them with grasses. The birds may roost, or rest and sleep, on cliff ledges and in trees away from the nest sites. When the birds are not breeding or nesting, they often fly down to grassy fields, farmland, rivers, streams, and lakeshores to search for food.

Threats. The northern bald ibis lives in scattered flocks in parts of northern and western Africa. They also live in some countries in the Middle East. The bird's numbers have been falling for centuries, for reasons that biologists do not fully understand. This *species* (type) is known to have lived during historical times in much of southern Europe— areas where it is now absent.

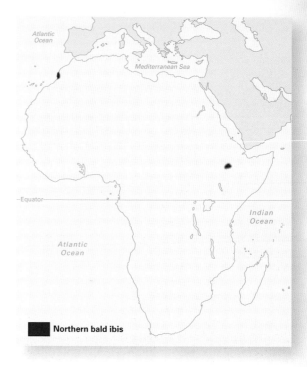

Northern bald ibis

Biologists blame the more recent population declines on a number of factors, which vary depending on location. In Morocco, for example, disturbances from construction and farming have harmed ibis *habitats* (the kind of place an animal normally lives in). In Syria, by contrast, the main threats have come from hunting and habitat destruction caused by the overgrazing of livestock and collecting of firewood. In Turkey, northern bald ibis populations have declined because of poisoning by insecticides. In Jordan, many ibises have been electrocuted when trying to roost on electric power pylons.

The largest remaining population of wild northern bald ibises lives in Morocco, where management and conservation efforts have boosted their numbers. Conservationists have bred some northern bald ibises in captivity and released the offspring into certain places in the wild, including Spain.

Northern bald ibises forage in large flocks, pecking the ground with their long beaks.

Spheniscus demersus

Conservation status: Endangered

The African, or jackass, penguin is the only *species* (type) of penguin that breeds on this continent. African penguins live in colonies in far southern Africa—mainly on the coasts of South Africa and Namibia and on several small islands off the coasts of these countries. They have also been recorded as far north as Mozambique, on the continent's southeastern coast.

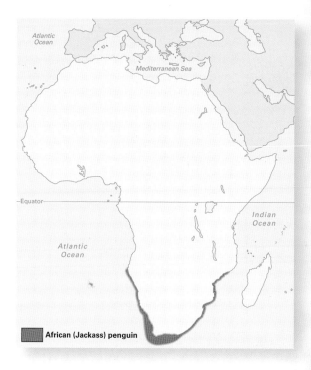

African (Jackass) penguin

Communication. African penguins are known by the alternate name of "jackass penguins" because of the loud, donkeylike calls they make. They make a "yell" sound to defend their territory from other penguins in the colony. They make a "bray" call to attract and communicate with their mates. They make a "haw" call when one member of a mated pair is on land and the other is in the water.

Appearance. Like most other penguins, the flightless African penguin is black on the back and white on the chest and belly. It averages about 18 inches (45 centimeters) tall.

Diet. African penguins spend most of their time in cold seawaters within 25 miles (40 kilometers) of the shore. As they swim, they search for small fish to eat, such as anchovies and sardines. They can swim as fast as 12 miles (20 kilometers) per hour, and they can dive as deep as 197 feet (60 meters).

Reproduction. African penguins come ashore to rest, *molt* (shed and replace their plumage), and breed. Pairs mate for life and return to the same breeding and nesting site every year. Females usually lay two eggs in burrows under boulders or bushes. The males and females take turns *incubating* the eggs (keeping them warm) for about 40 days. Both parents care for their young, which they feed with a mixture that they bring up from their stomach.

Threats. The wild population of African penguins has plummeted by 90 percent since the 1930's. The birds are endangered mainly because the animals they depend on for food have become harder to find. The huge catches of commercial fishing ships have depleted the anchovies and sardines the penguins prefer. Biologists believe that climate change has also contributed to the decline of these fish populations and to shifts in their *habitats* (living places). Penguin eggs were once a popular food, for people as well as cats, dogs, and other *invasive* (alien) *species* introduced to the bird's habitat.

Tourists have also been a problem. Their presence seems to disturb the penguins and reduce their breeding rate. Oil spills have severely harmed African penguin populations in the past, killing tens of thousands of the birds.

The government of South Africa has established nature reserves to protect penguin breeding sites. Captive breeding programs have helped build up penguin numbers.

African penguins sometimes compete with seals for breeding sites.

Indri indri

Conservation status: Endangered

The indri is the largest of the lemurs—long-tailed, furry mammals related to monkeys. All lemurs live in the island countries of Madagascar and Comoros, off the southeastern coast of Africa. The indri inhabits the rain forests of eastern Madagascar.

Appearance. Adult indris grow to a length of 28 inches (71 centimeters) and weigh from 15 to 22 pounds (7 to 10 kilograms). The indri has thick, silky, black-and-white fur that grows in different patterns and shades, depending on the location of the population. Their large, noticeable ears are black.

Daily life. Indris spend most of their time in trees, where they feed on leaves, flowers, and fruits during the day. They leap from tree to tree using their long, powerful hind legs. When they move down to the forest floor, they usually skip about on their hind legs, stretching their arms off to the side to keep their balance.

Indris communicate with each other using loud howls. Different howls in different settings may have various meanings—including information about an individual's reproductive status and territorial claims. Some howls are used to bring scattered members of a family group back together. The indri's call is so loud that it can be heard by people more than 1 mile (1.69 kilometer) away.

Families. An indri family group usually consists of two adults and their offspring. The adult female is typically larger and more *dominant* (higher ranking) than her male mate. She does most of the foraging to feed the young. The male defends the family's territory by marking it with urine and fluids from glands in his muzzle.

For its first four or five months, a baby indri rides on its mother's belly. Then it moves to her back. But being a baby indri can be very dan-

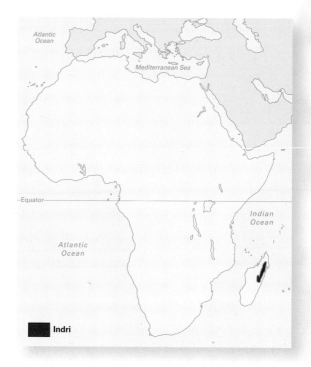

Indri

gerous! Biologists estimate that half of young indris die before they are 2 years old because of falls from trees or other injuries and illnesses.

The loss of an indri infant is serious for the survival of this *species* (type) because the indri reproduces so slowly. Females do not become sexually mature until they are about 9 years old, and then they are capable of reproducing only once every two or three years.

Threats. The indri is considered one of the most threatened primate species in the world. The main reason—aside from its slow reproductive rate—is the destruction of its rain forest *habitat* (living place). People cut down or burn the trees to get wood for fuel and construction and to make space for farmland. As the human population increases in Madagascar, so do the pressures on the rain forest. Some local people hunt the indri for its meat or its beautiful fur, which is used to decorate clothing.

The indri is known in Madagascar as the babakoto or ambalana. The word *indri* actually means *there it is.*

There are nine *species* (types) of colobus monkeys, all of which live in African forests south of the Sahara. They differ from most other monkeys by not having thumbs. Their tails, which are 20 to 39 inches (51 to 99 centimeters) long, are longer than their bodies. Different species have fur that may be black, black-and-white, red, or olive. In most cases, the hair on their forehead is parted down the middle.

Most colobus monkeys live in a variety of forested environments, including tropical rain forests, *montane* (mountain) forests, and forests along rivers. Although they frequently travel on the ground, colobus monkeys live mainly in trees. Their strong grip allows them to swing confidently from tree to tree. Colobus monkeys are also called "leaf monkeys" because they eat mainly leaves, though they sometimes eat fruit, flower buds, bark, and other parts of plants.

Colobus monkeys live in groups that range from about 3 to 80 members. Most groups consist of a few adult males and several adult females and their young. Some groups have only one adult male. Unlike black-and-white colobus monkeys, red colobus monkeys generally do not defend their home areas.

All colobus monkeys are threatened with extinction because of hunting for their beautiful fur and the clearing of their forest *habitats* (living places) for human settlements and agriculture. Some biologists consider red colobus monkeys to be the most endangered primate in Africa.

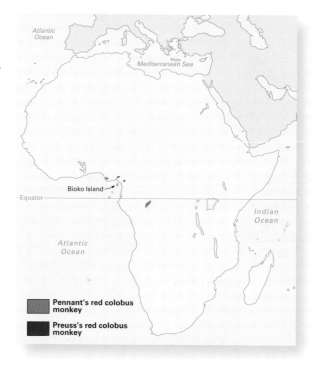

Pennant's red colobus monkey

Preuss's red colobus monkey

Pennant's red colobus monkey
Procolobus pennantii

Conservation status: Critically Endangered

The Pennant's red colobus monkey is found mostly in the large Niger River Delta, where the river empties into the Gulf of Guinea, an arm of the Atlantic Ocean. This region is one of the wettest places in Africa. It is also one of the most biologically diverse—that is, it contains a wide variety of plant and animal life. Pennant's red colobus monkeys also live along the Congo

River and on a small island called Bioko Island. Populations of the monkeys are isolated from one another because of the break-up of their forest habitat.

Troops. Red colobus monkeys advertise the boundaries of their territory with a variety of barks and chirps given by all members of the troop. Troops of Pennant's red colobus monkeys usually have many more female than male members. The females are likely to remain with the same troop throughout their lives. Males may move from group to group.

Threats. Hunting with shotguns and the destruction of their habitat led to a rapid decline of Pennant's red colobus populations beginning in the 1980's. Loggers removed many types of trees that the monkeys depend on for food. The lack of government controls on hunting and logging worsened the monkey's decline.

The loud cries and slow movements of the Pennant's red colobus monkey (left) make it an easy target for hunters.

The Preuss's red colobus monkey (above) is critically endangered despite protection in national parks.

Preuss's red colobus monkey
Procolobus preussi

Conservation status: Critically Endangered

The Preuss's red colobus monkey ranges farther south along the West African coast than its Pennant's red colobus cousin—from southeastern Nigeria into Cameroon. It lives in moist forests, some of which lie within protected national parks, such as Korup National Park in southwestern Cameroon.

Threats. Despite Korup's protection, the Preuss's red colobus monkey remains critically endangered because of decades of hunting and habitat degradation. The population has plummeted by about 80 percent in the past 30 years. Formerly large populations outside the national parks have disappeared.

The chimpanzee and the bonobo (formerly called the pygmy chimpanzee) live in the tropical forests of central Africa. The chimpanzee lives in isolated groups from Gambia in the west to Uganda in the east. The bonobo lives only in the Democratic Republic of the Congo.

Chimpanzee
Pan troglodytes
Conservation status: Endangered

Chimpanzees are highly social, intelligent animals. They live in groups that travel through the forest in search of fruits, leaves, nuts, seeds, and stems to eat. Chimps also eat birds' eggs and insects, and they sometimes kill and eat monkeys and other animals. Chimps communicate with each other with a variety of calls and cries.

Threats. Chimpanzees are the most abundant and widespread of the great apes (which also include gorillas and orangutans), but their populations are endangered. The main threat to these

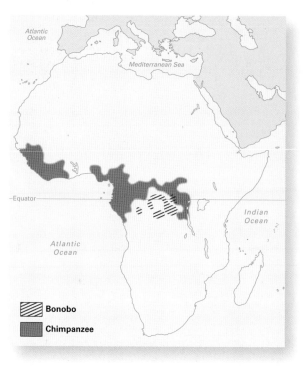

The chimpanzee (below) and bonobo (right) are members of the ape family. Like other apes, they have large brains and rank as the most intelligent animals next to humans.

animals is loss of *habitat* (living place) resulting from growing human populations. People cut and burn down the forest to clear land for agriculture. They build roads through chimpanzee habitat to reach logging and mining sites. *Poachers* (illegal hunters) kill chimps to get *bushmeat* (meat from wild animals), which is sold in urban markets and restaurants. Poachers also kill adult chimps to capture their infants, which are sold as pets.

As farms, roads, and other human developments expand into forest areas, there is increased contact between chimpanzees and people. This contact can result in certain diseases, such as deadly Ebola hemorrhagic fever, being transmitted between the *species* (types).

Many chimpanzees live in protected national parks, and government laws ban their killing or capture. But these laws are not always enforced. The illegal bushmeat market continues to flourish. And diseases do not stop at national park boundaries.

Bonobo
Pan paniscus
Conservation status: Endangered

Bonobos are more slender than chimpanzees, with smaller heads, flatter faces, and longer legs. Like chimpanzees, bonobos face a major threat from poaching for the bushmeat market, even in protected wildlife reserves. Bonobos are also threatened by the growth of the human population and habitat changes related to agriculture, logging, and mining. Government corruption and political instability in central Africa are major roadblocks to successful conservation.

Conservation organizations are working to educate local people about the benefits of protecting bonobos and chimpanzees. For example, Lola Ya Bonobo is a bonobo sanctuary and education center in Kinshasa, the capital of the Democratic Republic of the Congo. Thousands of schoolchildren and other local people visit this center every year.

Gorillas are social, intelligent, and fierce-looking but normally gentle animals. They are also critically endangered. There are two *species* (types) of gorilla—the western gorilla and the eastern gorilla. The western gorilla is divided into the western lowland and Cross River *subspecies*. (A subspecies is a group of organisms that are more closely related to each other than to other members of their species.) The eastern gorilla is divided into lowland and mountain subspecies.

Western lowland gorilla
Gorilla gorilla

Conservation status: Critically Endangered

Western lowland gorillas live in the forests of tropical western Africa, from Cameroon to Angola. They eat such plant food as leaves, shoots, and fruits. They live in groups made up of a large, *dominant* adult male—the leader—and several adult females with their offspring. The dominant male is called a "silverback"

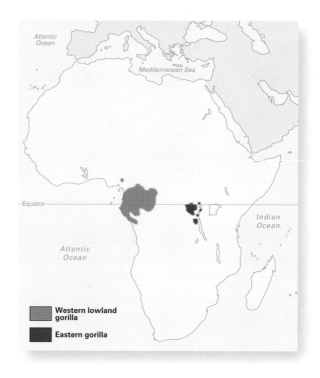

Western lowland
gorilla

Eastern gorilla

A Western lowland gorilla displays the greyish-silver fur that marks him as a dominant male.

because of the grayish-silver fur that becomes mixed with the black fur on his back as he ages.

Threats. Western lowland gorillas are threatened by the loss of their *habitat* (living place) to agriculture, logging, and mining; the spread of human diseases; and *poaching* (illegal hunting) for *bushmeat* (meat from wild animals). Gorilla populations have fallen much more than chimpanzee populations. Gorillas have a harder time recovering from declines because they breed so slowly. Biologists estimate that a female gorilla typically gives birth to an infant that survives to adulthood only once every four to six years.

Gorilla populations are also in trouble because conservation laws are often not enforced. Governments in the animal's habitats have long been plagued by corruption, political instability, and war. Some government officials have even participated in illegal trading in gorilla skulls, hands, and other body parts.

Silverback males are very protective of their females and offspring. They tend to rush to the defense of any members of their group being threatened by a hunter. That makes it easy for hunters to kill silverbacks.

Like other kinds of gorilla, the Eastern mountain gorilla (above) has no enemies except human beings.

Eastern gorilla
Gorilla beringei

Conservation status: Critically Endangered

Eastern gorillas live to the east of the western gorilla's *range* (area in which an animal naturally occurs) in the Democratic Republic of the Congo, Rwanda, and Uganda. The mountain subspecies is found in the high forests of the Virunga volcanoes, surrounded by farmland, and in a hilly area in Uganda. The lowland subspecies lives in low-altitude forests in the region. The appearance and behaviors of the eastern gorilla are similar to those of the western gorilla, though the eastern apes usually live in larger groups than their western cousins do.

Eastern gorilla populations face the same main threats as western populations do. Biologists believe that fewer than 1,000 eastern mountain gorillas exist in the wild.

Acinonyx jubatus

Conservation status: Vulnerable

The sleek, powerful cheetah is the fastest land animal in the world, capable of running as fast as 70 miles (110 kilometers) per hour for short distances. This predator is built for speed—with a small head, long legs, thin waist, and flexible spine. The cheetah's claws grip the ground for better traction, unlike the claws of other cats, which retract into the toes. The cheetah's long tail provides balance when the cat makes sharp turns while chasing prey.

Habitat. Cheetahs live mainly on the grassy plains of eastern and southern Africa. Some can be found in African dry forests, semidesert areas, mountains, or *savannas* (grassy plains with only a few, scattered trees). The current *range* of the cheetah (area in which it naturally occurs) is much smaller than its historic range. Scientists believe that cheetahs inhabit less than a quarter of the range they used to have in Africa. They have vanished from most of northern and western Africa. They have also disappeared from a former range running from the Middle East into central Asia and India. Biologists estimate that only 7,500 to 10,000 cheetahs remain in the wild.

Threats. The cheetah's numbers have plummeted for several reasons. People hunt cheetahs for their yellow-brown coat with black spots, which is sold illegally. Cheetah cubs are also sold illegally as pets on the international black market.

Much of the animal's grassland *habitat* (living place) has been turned into agricultural, mining, industrial, and residential *developments*. Cheetah habitats that were once connected are now separated by these human developments, limiting the cheetah's ability to move to a better environment. The decline in cheetah numbers is also linked to a decline in the numbers of their prey animals, such as gazelle. When their natural prey is scarce,

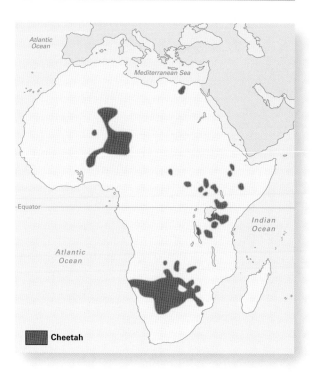

Cheetah

some cheetahs turn to livestock as a source of food. Ranchers kill cheetahs that they view as threats to their livestock.

Cheetahs also face natural threats. For example, lions are known to capture and eat young cheetahs. Many biologists believe that natural causes—probably a decline in their prey resulting from climate change—led to the near extinction of cheetahs about 10,000 years ago. Inbreeding among the few remaining individuals weakened the cheetah's *immune system* (the body's defense against disease and other harm) over time, making the animals more vulnerable to disease.

Conservation. Captive breeding programs are attempting to maintain the *species's* (type's) remaining genetic variation. A number of conservation programs are aimed at other problems plaguing cheetahs. In Namibia, a program called the Cheetah Conservation Fund provides ranchers with guard dogs to protect their livestock. This program has reduced the number of cheetahs killed by ranchers.

A mother cheetah and her cub stay together for up to 18 months while the cub learns to hunt.

Lycaon pictus

Conservation status: Endangered

The scientific name of the African wild dog, *Lycaon pictus*, means *painted wolflike animal* in Greek. The "painted" part of that name refers to the multicolored coat of this *canid* (animal in the dog family). The splashes of yellow, brown, grey, black, and white look like an abstract painting. The pattern of these color blotches differs from animal to animal, providing scientists with an easy means of identifying individuals. The African wild dog is also known as the African hunting dog.

Appearance. Other than its coat, the most distinctive trait of the African wild dog is its big round ears. These ears allow the dogs to hear the calls of other members of their pack when the pack is spread out over a wide area. The big ears also help the dogs release heat when they're running under the hot sun of the African plains. Other traits of the African wild dog are the long legs and bushy tail on its thin, muscular body. It also has powerful jaws and teeth.

Pack life. African wild dogs live in pack of usually 10 to 40 animals. A *dominant* (high-ranking) adult male and female, forming a breeding pair, lead each pack. The dominant female gives birth in a den to a litter of 6 to 16 pups. The pack assists in grooming, feeding, and protecting the litter.

The pack travels long distances in search of prey. Pack members hunt during the day, often surrounding their victim and chasing it until it becomes exhausted. Their prey includes antelopes, gazelles, wildebeests, and zebras.

Habitat. African wild dogs are found today mostly in small, widely spaced populations within wildlife parks and reserves in southern and eastern Africa. They formerly lived throughout sub-Saharan Africa. They can adapt to many different kinds of environments, and their *habitats* (living places) include grassy

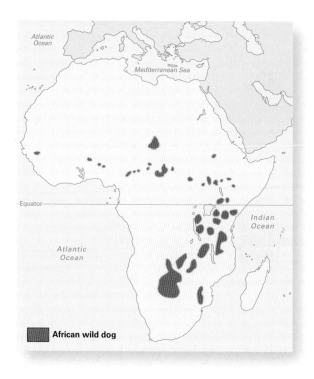

African wild dog

plains, bushy *savannas* (grassy plains), upland forests, and semidesert areas.

Threats. As the human population has grown—and as wild dog habitat has been broken up by roads, buildings, and farms—contact has increased between the wild dogs and people and their domestic dogs. Local people often kill the wild dogs they encounter. Infectious diseases have also spread from people and their dogs to the wild dogs. These diseases have been a major cause of the drop in the number of African wild dogs.

Another cause of the dog's decline is competition from hyenas, which live in the same habitats. Hyenas prey on many of the same hoofed animals as the wild dogs do. Finally, lions prey on wild dogs and their pups. Although many wild dogs live in reserves under legal protection, the conservation laws in these reserves are often not enforced.

The African wild dog once roamed in large numbers throughout much of Africa.

Canis simensis

Conservation status: Endangered

The Ethiopian wolf may be the most endangered *canid* (member of the dog family). This *species* (type) exists in small, scattered populations in six or seven mountain ranges in Ethiopia. Scientists estimate that there may be fewer than 500 of the wolves.

Appearance. The Ethiopian wolf looks more like a coyote than the gray wolf found in North America. It has the coyote's thin body, long legs, and long, narrow muzzle, rather than the gray wolf's more robust build. Its fur is mostly tawny brown, with a white chin and chest. During the breeding season, the fur of females becomes more yellowish.

Pack life. These canids live in packs made up of from 3 to 13 adults and their offspring. The packs are territorial, marking the boundaries of the areas they claim several times a day with scent and chasing away all intruders. Young males tend to remain within their group, but females usually leave their group to mate with males of other groups. This avoids inbreeding.

Females give birth to litters of two to six pups in underground dens. The pups stay in the den for about three weeks. Members of the pack closely guard the den and try to protect the pups from predators.

Habitat. Ethiopian wolves are found in such mountain *habitats* (living places) as alpine grasslands and heathlands. Alpine grasslands, also known as *montane* (mountain) grasslands, are grassy and shrubby places at high elevations. Heathlands, also known as moorlands, are open areas with short evergreen shrubs and few or no trees. Both these areas have many rodents, the wolves' main food. The wolves stalk and kill giant molerats and grass rats. They even dig these rats out of their burrows. Although Ethiopian wolves live in packs, they prefer to hunt and forage on their own.

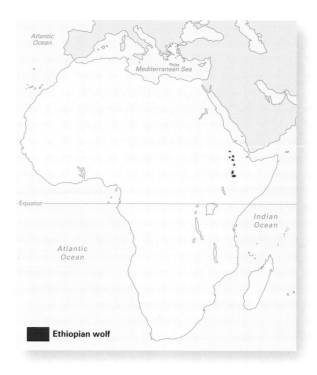

Ethiopian wolf

Threats. The habitats of the wolves are shrinking as the human population increasingly moves into these areas, replacing the natural vegetation with farmland. *Native* plant species (species that occur naturally in an area) are also destroyed by grazing livestock and the building of roads. Farmers and ranchers sometimes kill the wolves, viewing them as threats to their livestock.

Domestic dogs brought into wolf habitats by people pose serious threats to wolf populations in two ways. Diseases from domestic dogs, especially rabies and canine distemper, can spread to the wolves. And domestic dogs breed with the wolves, producing hybrid, or mixed, offspring that weaken the natural wolf gene pool—that is, the *genes* (hereditary material) of this species. Conservationists are working to educate local people about the need to protect the wolves—such as by sterilizing their dogs and vaccinating them against diseases. Some wolves have also been vaccinated against diseases.

In recent years, the Ethiopian wolf has been threatened by human conflict in its territory.

Diceros bicornis

Conservation status: Critically Endangered

The black rhinoceros is the more endangered of the two African rhino *species* (types), the other species being the white rhinoceros. The black rhino is smaller than the white rhino and has a pointed upper lip. The upper lip of the white rhino is squared. Despite their names, both the black and white rhino are almost the same bluish-gray color.

Horns. The black rhinoceros has two horns. The front horn—used for defense and digging—may be as long as 3.5 feet (1.1 meters). The rear horn is typically shorter. The digging horn is so strong that the rhino can use it to uproot bushes and small trees. The animal then feeds on the leaves and twigs of the uprooted plant. The horns grow throughout the animal's lifetime.

The horns consist of a fiberlike material similar to a mixture of hair and fingernails. The horn appears to be permanently joined to the rhinoceros's nose but can be torn out during fighting. The name rhinoceros comes from two Greek words and means *nose-horned*.

Habitat. Black rhinoceroses formerly existed in huge numbers throughout much of sub-Saharan Africa. Today, their population is greatly reduced and fragmented. Most of the rhinos live in reserves in South Africa and Namibia.

Threats. The growth and spread of the human population destroyed much of the black rhino's *habitat* (living place). Today, the rhinos are seriously threatened by *poachers* (illegal hunters), who kill the animals and sell their horns and other body parts. Rhino horns may sell at prices higher than the price of gold!

Some Asian people believe that powdered rhinoceros horn has healing powers, though no scientific evidence exists to support that belief. Asian people also use the skin, blood, and urine of rhinoceroses for healing purposes. Some people believe the horn has magical powers.

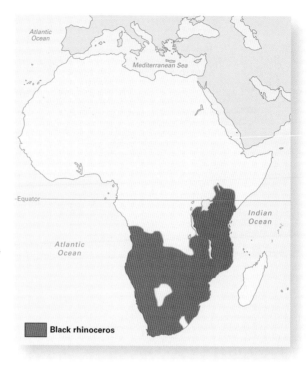

Black rhinoceros

People in the Middle East use the horn for the handles of ceremonial daggers.

Conservation. African countries have passed a number of laws to protect both black and white rhinoceroses from poachers. Many rhinos live in fenced sanctuaries or carefully guarded unfenced zones. Some wildlife officials have tried to reduce poaching by cutting off the horns of rhinoceroses. Many scientists, however, believe that tactic puts the animals in greater danger. Hornless rhinos are less able to protect themselves against such predators as lions and hyenas. Moreover, poachers still kill hornless rhinoceroses for other body parts, including the horn root.

Despite legal protections, the number of rhinoceroses killed by poachers hit a new annual record in South Africa in 2013—1,004. Most of the dead animals were white rhinos, which are much more numerous than black rhinos.

Some black rhinos have been sent to Australia and the United States to form breeding colonies for future repopulation in the wild.

Hexaprotodon liberiensis

Conservation status: Endangered

The pygmy hippopotamus is a smaller version of the common, or river, hippopotamus, with a few physical differences. The eyes of the pygmy hippopotamus are farther along the sides of the head, and their feet have less webbing between the toes. The pygmy hippopotamus weighs from 400 to 600 pounds (180 to 270 kilograms) and stands about 2.5 feet (76 centimeters) tall. By contrast, the common hippopotamus weighs from 2,500 to 3,000 pounds (1,130 to 1,400 kilograms) and stands about 5 feet (1.5 meters) tall. The pygmy hippopotamus has blackish skin.

Behavior. Pygmy hippopotamuses also differ from common hippopotamuses in their behaviors. They live in dense forests near streams, swamps, or other bodies of water and spend less time in the water than the larger hippos. Going into the water helps hippos keep cool in their hot, humid environment. Glands in their skin secrete a shiny brownish-red fluid, called "blood sweat," that helps protect the skin from the sun.

On land, the barrel-shaped animals plow through the dense vegetation of their *habitat* (living place), creating paths that they reuse in their travels. They sometimes take shelter in burrows made by other animals in riverbanks, enlarging the burrows so that they can fit inside. Pygmy hippos live alone or in pairs, rather than in herds like the bigger hippos.

Pygmy hippos eat leaves, roots, ferns, and fruits that grow near rivers and streams. In the forest, they may stand on their hind legs to reach food higher up in trees.

Habitat. Pygmy hippopotamuses live in western Africa. There are roughly 2,000 to 3,000 of these animals in the wild. The population is highest in Liberia, with fewer individuals in such countries as Guinea, Côte d'Ivoire, and Sierra Leone.

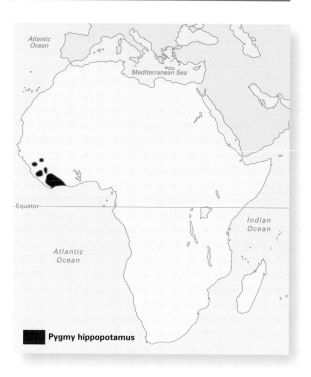

Pygmy hippopotamus

Threats. Killing pygmy hippopotamuses is illegal. But the laws protecting them are often not enforced because of corruption, war, or other problems. Africans shoot many pygmy hippos for food. African farmers also shoot many hippopotamuses to keep the animals from eating or trampling their crops.

Since the 1980's, much of this animal's forest habitat has disappeared as the human population has grown and spread. People have cut down the trees for timber and converted the forest into farmland, settlements, and other developments. Pygmy hippos are sensitive to any disturbances in their habitat, so these changes are harmful to the *species* (type).

Pygmy hippos breed well in zoos, and there are many individuals in captivity. This captive population may offer a source of animals for eventual release into the wild. However, conservationists warn that more action is needed to preserve the hippo's natural habitat in Africa.

A pygmy hippopotamus and her calf (between her legs) walk through tall grass seeking food.

Addax nasomaculatus

Conservation status: Critically Endangered

The addax is an antelope that lives in the deserts of northern Africa. It has developed many special *adaptations* to help it survive in its harsh environment. (An adaptation is a characteristic of an organism that makes it better able to survive and reproduce in its environment.) The addax can withstand high temperatures. It has splayed, or spread out, hooves that enable it to walk easily on soft sand—in much the same way that the wide bottom of a snowshoe makes it easier to walk on snow without sinking. The addax can go without water for long periods. It conserves water by producing urine that is highly concentrated, meaning that it contains little water. The animal gets almost all of its water from the coarse grasses, scrubby bushes, and other desert plants that it eats.

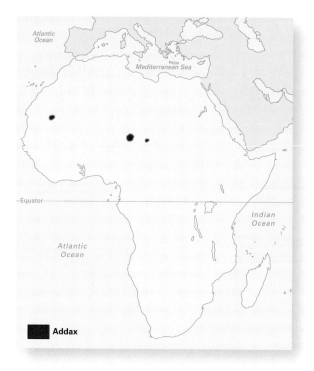

Addax

Appearance. The addax has short, glossy fur that changes color from winter to summer. Its body and neck are grayish-brown in winter and sandy to almost white in summer. There is a patch of chestnut-colored hair on the forehead. Both males and females have spiral horns that grow to about 4 feet (1.2 meters) in length.

Daily life. The addax wanders through its sandy *habitat* (living place) in herds made up of from 5 to 30 individuals. The herd is led by a *dominant* (high-ranking) male who may mate with several females. Addaxes are most active during the night. During the hottest times of the day, they often rest in the shade under trees.

Threats. The addax is in danger of extinction because of overhunting and habitat loss caused by human development. The animals are easy to kill because they move slowly. Local people value the meat and leather that they get from the addax.

Scientists estimate that the addax's population has decreased by more than 80 percent since about 1990. The total wild population may number only in the hundreds, with most survivors in Niger and Chad. Conservationists consider the addax and another antelope called the Dama gazelle to be the most endangered bovids, or members of the cattle family, living in the Sahara.

Addaxes face additional threats besides hunting and habitat loss. Four-wheel-drive vehicles used by tourists frighten the antelopes and may cause them to die of exhaustion as they run away. Droughts have reduced the already sparse plant life in addax's habitat, making it harder for the animals to find enough food.

Conservation. Some addax populations are protected within wildlife reserves, including the Yotvata Hai-Bar Nature Reserve in Israel. Approximately 2,000 addaxes live in captive populations around the world.

The addax has been widely hunted for its meat and hide.

Glossary

Adaptation A trait of an organism that makes it better able to survive and reproduce in its environment.

Bushmeat Meat obtained through the hunting of wild animals, especially meat taken from tropical forests by local people.

Canid An animal belonging to a biological family that includes dogs, wolves, and similar animals.

Carapace A shell or bony covering on the back or part of the back of turtles and other animals.

Deforestation The destruction or damage of forests, mainly by people to create farmland, harvest timber, and build structures.

Development Refers to farmland, cities, dams, roads, or other changes that damage or destroy the natural environment.

Dominant In terms of animal behavior, refers to a powerful individual who influences the behavior of other individuals.

Ecosystem A natural system made up of certain living organisms and their physical environment.

Estivation An inactive state that occurs in the life of some animals during hot, dry periods.

Gene A part of a cell that determines which characteristics living things inherit from their parents.

Genus A group of related organisms that is usually made up of two or more species.

Habitat The type of environment in which an organism lives.

Immune system The combination of cells, proteins, and tissues that defend an animal's body against disease and other harm.

Incubation Keeping eggs at the right temperature and condition to hatch.

Invertebrate An animal without a backbone.

Invasive species Animals, plants, and other living things that spread rapidly in new environments where there are few or no natural controls on their growth.

Larva An immature form of an insect or certain other animals.

Missing link A species that was a link between an earlier and later species.

Molt To shed feathers, skin, hair, shell, antlers, or other growths, before a new growth.

Montane Of, having to do with, or inhabiting mountains.

Native species A species that occurs naturally in a region.

Poaching The illegal killing of an animal.

Queen ant Female in a colony that breeds.

Range The area in which certain plants or animals live or naturally occur.

Savanna A grassy plain with few, scattered trees.

Sediment Soil, stones, and other matter that flows into a body of water and becomes suspended in the water or settles to the bottom.

Species A group of animals or plants that have certain permanent characteristics in common and are able to interbreed.

Steppe A level, treeless plain in southeastern Europe and parts of Asia.

Subspecies A group of organisms that are more closely related to each other than to other members of the same species.

Venom The poison made in the body of certain animals.

Viviparous Bearing live young as opposed to laying eggs.

Books

Animal Encyclopedia: 2,500 Animals with Photos, Maps, and More! Washington, DC: National Geographic, 2012. Print.

Hammond, Paula. *The Atlas of Endangered Animals: Wildlife Under Threat Around the World.* Tarrytown, NY: Marshall Cavendish, 2010. Print.

Hoare, Ben, and Tom Jackson. *Endangered Animals.* New York: DK Pub., 2010. Print.

Lourie, Peter. *The Manatee Scientists: Saving Vulnerable Species.* Boston: Houghton Mifflin Harcourt, 2011. Print.

Montgomery, Sy, and Nic Bishop. *Chasing Cheetahs: The Race to Save Africa's Fastest Cats.* Boston: Houghton Mifflin Harcourt, 2014. Print.

Websites

"African Wildlife." *BBC Nature.* BBC, 2014. Web. 21 May2014.

African Wildlife Foundation. African Wildlife Foundation, n.d. Web. 21 May 2014.

"Animal Conservation." *National Geographic.* National Geographic Society, 2014. Web. 21 May 2014.

Arkive. Wildscreen, 2014. Web. 14 May 2014.

"Endangered Species." *BBC Bitesize Science.* BBC, 2014. Web. 21 May 2014.

"Especies Fact Sheets." *Kids' Planet.* Defenders of Wildlife, n.d. Web. 14 May 2014.

Tregaskis, Shiona. "The world's extinct and endangered species – interactive map." *The Guardian.* Guardian News and Media Limited, 3 Sept. 2012. Web. 14 May 2014.

Organizations *for helping endangered animals*

Alaska Wildlife Adoption
By adopting an animal at the Alaska Wildlife Conservation Center, you can enjoy animal parenthood without all the work.
http://www.alaskawildlife.org/support/alaska-wildlife-adoption/

Defenders of Wildlife
Founded in 1947, Defenders of Wildlife is a major national conservation organization focused on wildlife and habitat conservation.
http://www.defenders.org/take-action

National Geographic – Big Cats Initiative
National Geographic, along with Dereck and Beverly Joubert, launched the Big Cats Initiative to raise awareness and implement change to the dire situation facing big cats.
http://animals.nationalgeographic.com/animals/big-cats-initiative/

National Geographic – The Ocean Initiative
National Geographic's Ocean Initiative helps identify and support individuals and organizations that are using creative and entrepreneurial approaches to marine conservation.
http://ocean.nationalgeographic.com/ocean/about-ocean-initiative

National Wildlife Federation – Adoption Center
Symbolically adopt your favorite species and at the same time support the National Wildlife Federation's important work protecting wildlife and connecting people to nature.
http://www.shopnwf.org/Adoption-Center/index.cat

Neighbor Ape
Neighbor Ape strives to conserve the habitat of wild chimpanzees in southeastern Senegal, to protect the chimpanzees themselves, and to provide for the wellbeing of the Senegalese people who have traditionally lived in the area alongside these chimpanzees.
http://www.globalgiving.org/donate/10235/neighbor-ape/

Smithsonian National Zoo – Adopt a Species
The Adopt a Species program supports the National Zoo's extraordinary work in the conservation and care of the world's rarest animals.
http://nationalzoo.si.edu/support/adoptspecies/

World Wildlife Fund
World Wildlife Fund works in 100 countries and is supported by over 1 million members in the United States and close to 5 million globally.
http://www.worldwildlife.org/how-to-help

Index

Acknowledgments

The publishers acknowledge the following sources for illustrations. Credits read from top to bottom, left to right, on their respective pages. All maps, charts, and diagrams were prepared by the staff unless otherwise noted.

COVER © Peter Blackwell, Nature Picture Library; © Chris Matisson, Alamy Images
4 © Chris Matisson, Alamy Images
7 © Alex Wild, Visuals Unlimited
8 © Joel Sartore, National Geographic/Alamy Images
9 © Shem Compion, Getty Images
11 © Oceanwide Images
13 © John P. Clare
15 © Daniel Heuclin, Andrew Murray, Nature Picture Library
16 © David Kjaer, Nature Picture Library
18 © Christophe Courteau, Nature Picture Library
19 © Ryan M. Bolton, Alamy Images
21 © Juniors Bildarchiv, Alamy Images
23 © James Clarke, Alamy Images
25 © FLPA/Alamy Images
27 © Renato Granieri, Alamy Images
28 © Drew T. Cronin, Drexel University
29 © Dr. Joshua Linder
30 © Shutterstock
31 © Anup Shah, Nature Picture Library
32 © Anup Shah, Getty Images
33 © Ralph H. Bendjebar, Danita Delimont Photography/Alamy Images
35 © Steve Bloom, Alamy Images
37 © Tony Heald, Nature Picture Library
39 © Anup Shah, Nature Picture Library
41 © Ann & Steve Toon, Alamy Images
43 © Michael Fairchild, Getty Images
45 © blickwinkel/Alamy Images

DATE DUE

SEP

HISTORICAL STATISTICS OF THE SOUTH
1790-1970

HISTORICAL STATISTICS OF THE SOUTH
1790-1970

A Compilation of State-level Census Statistics for the Sixteen States of

Alabama
Arkansas
Delaware
Florida
Georgia
Kentucky
Louisiana
Maryland

Mississippi
North Carolina
Oklahoma
South Carolina
Tennessee
Texas
Virginia
West Virginia

By

Donald B. Dodd

and

Wynelle S. Dodd

The University of Alabama Press

University, Alabama

TABLE OF CONTENTS

PREFACE

Historical Statistics of the South resulted from repeated frustration in dealing with several aspects of census research which include: the sparsity of complete sets of census materials; the time involved in compiling workable statistics for a number of consecutive enumerations; and the difficulty in identifying the nature of statistics due to changing definitions. To counter some of these problems, the authors compiled state-level census data available for a significant number of consecutive decades and listed these items by years under the individual states. Hopefully this compilation and organization will encourage the use of trend data by the non-specialist as well as expediting census research for the specialist.

Explanations of terms are in the Glossary of Terms. Footnotes relate to the source of the information. Items which relate to per cent of a total (items 4, 35, 37, 39, and 42 of the General Population, Agriculture, and Manufacturing Statistics, 1790-1970) refer to the individual state's percentage of the national total.

No attempt to draw inferences from the data has been made. However, the data have potential for correlative and inferential statistics. The authors intend to include correlative and inferential tables in future publications.

Individuals who were helpful to the authors in compiling this book include: Mrs. Jessie Cobb, Mrs. Frances Macon, Mrs. Annie Lee Mills, and Mrs. Frances Clark of the staff of Alabama Archives and History; Mr. George Strong, Statistical Reporting Service, Montgomery, Alabama; and Dr. Joseph H. Yeager, Agricultural Economics, Auburn University at Auburn. The U.S. Bureau of the Census also assisted by expediting the delivery of appropriate schedules of the 1970 Census.

In this and other projects, Mr. Richard Pastorett, Librarian, Auburn University at Montgomery, has rendered invaluable aid.

Due to the complexity of the changes in the census enumerations during the past 180 years, as well as the bulk of statistical materials, there no doubt will be errors. Subsequent editions will correct errors noted by readers and incorporate helpful suggestions. Recommendations and comments should be sent to the authors in care of:

University of Alabama Press
Drawer 2877
University, Alabama 35486

HISTORICAL STATISTICS OF THE SOUTH
1790-1970

General Population, Agriculture, and Manufacturing Statistics, 1790–1970

ALABAMA

Item No.	1790 (or 1789)	1800	1810	1820	1830	1840	1850	1860	1870*
1. Population[1, 50]	...	1,250[a]	9,046[a]	127,901	309,527	590,756	771,623	964,201	996,992
2. Decennial rates of increase in population over preceding census[2, 50]	...	...	623.7	1,313.9	142.0	90.9	30.6	25.0	3.4
3. Increase in population over previous census[1, 3, 50]	...	...	7,796	118,855	181,626	281,229	180,867	192,578	32,791
4. Percent distribution of population[4]	...	...	0.1	1.3	2.4	3.5	3.3	3.1	2.6
5. Population per square mile of land area[5, 6, 50]	...	...	...	...	...	...	15.0	18.8	19.4
6. Membership of House of Representatives at each apportionment[7]	...	...	1	3	5	7	7	6	8
7. White population[8, 9, 10, 51]	...	733[b]	6,422[b]	85,451	190,406	335,185	426,514	526,271	521,384
8. Percentage increase in white population over preceding census[9, 10, 11, 51]	...	...	776.1	1,230.6	122.8	76.0	27.2	23.4	-0.9
9. Negro population[8, 9, 10, 51]	...	517[b]	2,624[b]	42,450	119,121	255,571	345,109	437,770	475,510
10. Percentage increase in Negro population over preceding census[9, 10, 11, 12, 13, 50]	...	...	407.5	1,517.7	180.6	114.5	35.0	26.8	8.6
11. Number of slaves in the area enumerated in 1790 and in the added area[14]	...	494[a]	2,565[a]	41,879	117,549	253,532	342,844	435,080	...
12. Urban population[15, 50]	...	...	...	...	3,194	12,672	35,179	48,901	62,700
13. Percent urban increase over preceding census[15, 50]	...	...	...	...	...	296.7	177.6	39.0	28.2
14. Rural population[15, 50]	...	1,250[a]	9,046[a]	127,901	306,333	578,084	736,444	915,300	934,292
15. Percent rural increase over preceding census[15, 50]	...	...	623.7	1,313.9	139.5	88.7	27.4	24.3	2.1
16. Percent of urban to total population[15, 50]	...	...	...	...	1.0	2.1	4.6	5.1	6.3
17. Percent of rural to total population[15, 50]	...	100.0	100.0	100.0	99.0	97.9	95.4	94.9	93.7
18. Number of farms[16, 52]	...	...	...	...	...	...	41,964	55,128	67,382
19. Acres in farms[16, 52]	...	...	...	...	...	...	12,137,681	19,104,545	14,961,178
20. Acres improved land in farms[17]	...	...	...	...	...	...	4,435,614	6,385,724	5,062,204
21. Cropland harvested, acres[16, 53]	...	...	...	...	...	...	...	...	...
22. Percentage increase in farm population[17, 18]	...	...	...	...	...	...	...	25.0	3.4
23. Percentage increase in number of farms[16, 17]	...	...	...	...	...	...	...	31.4	22.2
24. Percentage increase of land in farms[16, 17]	...	...	...	...	...	...	...	57.4	-21.7
25. Percentage increase of improved land in farms[17]	...	...	...	...	...	...	...	44.0	-20.7

General Population, Agriculture, and Manufacturing Statistics, 1790-1970

ALABAMA

1880	1890	1900	1910	1920	1930	1940	1950	1960	1970
1,262,505	1,513,401	1,828,697	2,138,093	2,348,174	2,646,248	2,832,961	3,061,743	3,266,740	3,444,165
26.6	19.9	20.8	16.9	9.8	12.7	7.1	8.1	6.7	5.4
265,513	250,512	315,680	309,396	210,081	298,074	186,713	228,782	204,997	177,425
2.5	2.4	2.4	2.3	2.2	2.1	2.1	2.0	1.8	. . .
24.6	29.5	35.7	41.7	45.8	51.8	55.5	59.9	64.0	67.9
8	9	9	10	10	9	9	9	8	7
662,185	833,718	1,001,152	1,228,832	1,447,032	1,700,844	1,849,097	2,079,591	2,283,609	2,533,831
27.0	25.9	20.1	22.7	17.8	17.5	8.7	12.5	9.8	11.0
600,103	678,489	827,307	908,282	900,652	944,834	983,290	979,617	980,271	903,467
26.2	13.1	21.9	9.8	-0.8	4.9	4.0	-0.4	. . .	-8.1
. . .	. . .	. . .	. . .	. . .	. . .	. . .	. . .	. . .	. . .
68,518	152,235	216,714	370,431	509,317	744,273	855,941	1,228,209[c] 1,340,937[d]	1,689,417[c] 1,791,721[d]	2,011,941
9.3	122.2	42.4	70.9	37.5	46.1	15.0	43.5[c] . . .[d]	37.6[c] 33.6[d]	12.3
1,193,987	1,361,166	1,611,983	1,767,662	1,838,857	1,901,975	1,977,020	1,833,534[c] 1,720,806[d]	1,577,323[c] 1,475,019[d]	1,432,224
27.8	14.0	18.4	9.7	4.0	3.4	3.9	-7.3[c] . . .[d]	-14.0[c] -14.3[d]	-2.9
5.4	10.1	11.9	17.3	21.7	28.1	30.2	40.1[c] 43.8[d]	51.7[c] 54.8[d]	58.4
94.6	89.9	88.1	82.7	78.3	71.9	69.8	59.9[c] 56.2[d]	48.3[c] 45.2[d]	41.6
135,864	157,772	223,220	262,901	256,099	257,395	231,746	211,512	115,788[e]	86,000
18,855,334	19,853,000	20,685,427	20,732,312	19,576,856	17,554,635	19,143,391	20,888,784	16,542,730[e]	14,700,000
6,375,706	7,698,343	8,654,991	9,693,581	9,893,407	. . .	. . .	. . .	. . .	. . .
5,048,506	5,444,261	6,714,786	7,205,239	7,266,357	7,113,937	7,111,717	5,729,421	3,715,251[e]	2,685,000
26.6	19.9	20.8	16.9	9.8	0.3	. . .	. . .	. . .	. . .
101.6	16.1	41.5	17.8	-2.6	0.5	10.0	-8.7	-45.2[e]	. . .
26.0	5.3	4.2	0.2	-5.6	-10.3	9.0	9.1	-20.8[e]	. . .
25.9	20.7	12.4	12.0	2.1	. . .	. . .	. . .	. . .	. . .

3

General Population, Agriculture, and Manufacturing Statistics, 1790-1970—ALABAMA (Cont.)

Item No.	1790 (or 1789)	1800	1810	1820	1830	1840	1850	1860	1870*
26. Average acreage per farm[16]	...	...	...	...	...	...	289.2	346.5	222.0
27. Percentage increase in cropland harvested[16]	...	...	...	...	...	...	...	...	...
28. Value of farms, dollars[16]	...	...	...	...	...	...	64,323,224	175,824,622	54,191,229
29. Value of farms, percent increase[16]	...	...	...	...	...	...	...	173.3	-69.2
30. Average value per farm, dollars[16]	...	...	...	...	...	...	1,533	3,189	804
31. Farms operated by owners[19, 20, 21, 22, 23, 24]	...	...	...	...	...	...	...	...	...
32. Value of livestock on farms, dollars[25, 26, 27, 54]	...	...	...	...	...	...	21,690,112	43,411,711	21,352,076[g]
33. Average value of livestock per farm, dollars[25, 26, 27, 52, 54]	...	...	...	...	...	...	517	787	317[g]
34. Production of cotton in commercial bales[28, 29, 30, 31, 53]	...	...	...	...	...	...	564,429	989,955	429,482
35. Percent of total production of cotton[28, 29, 30, 31, 53]	...	...	...	...	...	...	22.9	18.4	14.3
36. Production of corn in bushels[32, 33, 34, 35, 53]	...	...	...	...	...	...	28,754,048	33,226,282	16,977,948
37. Percent of total production of corn[32, 33, 34, 35, 53]	...	...	...	...	...	...	4.9	4.0	2.2
38. Production of tobacco in pounds[36, 37, 38, 53]	...	...	...	...	...	...	164,990	232,914	152,742
39. Percent of total production of tobacco[36, 37, 38, 53]	...	...	...	...	...	...	0.1	0.1	0.1
40. Production of rice in pounds[39]	...	...	...	...	...	...	2,312,252	493,465	222,945
41. Production of rice in bushels[40, 41]	...	...	...	...	...	...	...	...	...
42. Percent of total production of rice[39, 40, 41]	...	...	...	...	...	...	1.1	0.3	0.3
43. Number of manufacturing establishments[42, 43, 44, 45, 46, 55]	...	...	...	...	...	...	1,026	1,459	2,188
44. Capital of manufacturing establishments[42, 43, 44]	...	...	...	...	...	...	3,450,606	9,098,181	5,714,032
45. Average number of wage earners[42, 43, 44, 45, 46, 55]	...	...	...	...	...	...	4,936	7,889	8,248
46. Total wages[42, 43, 45, 46, 55]	...	...	...	...	...	...	1,105,824	2,132,940	2,227,968
47. Cost of materials used in manufacturing[42, 43, 44, 45, 46, 55]	...	...	...	...	...	...	2,224,960	5,489,963	7,592,837
48. Value of manufactured product[42, 43, 44, 45, 46]	...	...	...	...	...	...	4,528,876	10,588,566	13,040,644

a. Population of those parts of Alabama included in Mississippi Territory as then constituted.
b. Census corrected by reference to counties constituting present state area.
c. Previous urban/rural definition. Rural included population residing outside of incorporated places having 2,500 inhabitants or more.
d. Current urban/rural definition. Urban includes those residing in urban-fringe areas and in unincorporated places of 2,500 or more.
e. For 1959
f. Includes part owners
g. Values in gold
h. Computed on data available
i. Less than .1%
j. For 1967
k. Based on a sampling of farms

*The 1870 Census of population is considered incomplete in the Southern states.

1880	1890	1900	1910	1920	1930	1940	1950	1960	1970
138.8	125.8	92.7	78.9	76.4	68.2	82.6	98.8	142.9[e]	...
...	7.8	23.3	7.3	0.8	-2.1	...	-19.4	-35.1[e]	...
78.954,648	111,051,390	134,618,183	288,253,591	543,657,755	502,370,806	408,782,488	1,017,075,000[k]	1,479,820,000[e,k]	...
45.7	40.7	21.2	114.1	88.6	-7.6	-18.6	148.8[k]	45.5[e,k]	...
581	704	603	1,096	2,123	1,952	1,764	4,809[k]	12,780[e,k]	...
72,215	81,141	94,346	103,929[f]	107,089[f]	90,372[f]	95,107[f]	123,463[f]	83,539[f,e]	...
23,787,681	30,776,730	36,105,799	65,594,834	112,824,748	75,098,775	73,915,224	154,286,965	184,419,735[e]	292,983,000
175	195	162	250	441	292	319	729	1,593[e]	3,407
699,654	915,210	1,106,840	1,129,527	718,163	1,312,963	772,711	824,290	683,491	507,000
12.2	12.2	11.6	10.6	6.3	9.0	6.7	5.3	4.9[h]	5.0
25,451,278	30,072,161	35,053,047	30,695,737	43,699,100	35,683,874	31,028,109	40,972,309	62,580,000	12,535,000
1.4	1.4	1.3	1.2	1.9	1.7	1.3	1.5	1.5	.3
452,426	162,430	311,950	90,572	2,031,235	357,093	295,776	355,574	491,741	892,000
0.1	...	...	...	0.1	...	...	...	...	* *[i]
810,889	399,270	926,946	...	...	...	...	...	...	...
...	...	...	5,170	14,279	1,857	9,864	...	...	...
0.7	0.3	0.3	...	...	...	...	...	...	...
2,070	2,977	5,602	3,398	3,654	2,848	2,052)			4,951[j]
9,668,008	46,122,571	70,370,081	173,180,000	455,593,000	...	...)			
10,019	31,137	52,902	72,148	107,159	119,559	116,800)			288,800[j]
2,500,504	10,799,747	15,130,419	27,284,000	99,066,000	102,005,000	92,018,000)	See following table		1,602,800,000[j]
8,545,520	28,432,281	44,098,671	83,442,000	300,664,000	302,253,000	327,287,000)			3,956,400,000[j]
13,565,504	51,226,605	80,741,449	145,962,000	492,731,000	560,378,000	574,671,000)			...

General Population, Agriculture, and Manufacturing Statistics, 1790–1970

ARKANSAS

Item No.	1790 (or 1789)	1800	1810	1820	1830	1840	1850	1860	1870*
1. Population[1, 50]	...	...	1,062	14,273	30,388	97,574	209,897	435,450	484,471
2. Decennial rates of increase in population over preceding census[2, 50]	...	...	...	1,244.0	112.9	221.1	115.1	107.5	11.3
3. Increase in population over previous census[1, 3, 50]	...	...	...	14,273	16,115	67,186	112,323	225,553	49,021
4. Percent distribution of population[4]	...	...	...	0.1	0.2	0.6	0.9	1.4	1.3
5. Population per square mile of land area[5, 6, 50]	...	...	...	...	...	...	4.0	8.3	9.2
6. Membership of House of Representatives at each apportionment[7]	...	...	...	...	1	1	2	3	4
7. White population[8, 9, 10, 51]	...	...	924[a]	12,597	25,671	77,174	162,189	324,143	362,115
8. Percentage increase in white population over preceding census[9, 10, 11, 12, 13, 51]	...	...	...	1,263.3	103.8	200.6	110.2	99.9	11.7
9. Negro population[8, 9, 10, 51]	...	...	138[a]	1,676	4,717	20,400	47,708	111,259	122,169
10. Percentage increase in Negro population over preceding census[9, 10, 11, 12, 13, 51]	...	...	...	1,114.5	181.4	332.5	133.9	133.2	9.8
11. Number of slaves in the area enumerated in 1790 and in the added area[14]	...	...	136[b]	1,617	4,576	19,935	47,100	111,115	...
12. Urban population[15, 50]	...	...	...	...	...	...	...	3,727	12,380
13. Percent urban increase over preceding census[15, 50]	...	...	...	...	...	...	...	...	232.2
14. Rural population[15, 50]	...	...	1,062	14,273	30,388	97,574	209,897	431,723	472,091
15. Percent rural increase over preceding census[15, 50]	...	...	...	1,244.0	112.9	221.1	115.1	105.7	9.4
16. Percent of urban to total population[15, 50]	...	...	...	...	...	...	...	0.9	2.6
17. Percent of rural to total population[15, 50]	...	...	100.0	100.0	100.0	100.0	100.0	99.1	97.4
18. Number of farms[16, 52]	...	...	...	...	...	...	17,758	39,004	49,424
19. Acres in farms[16, 52]	...	...	...	...	...	...	2,598,214	9,573,706	7,597,296
20. Acres improved land in farms[17]	...	...	...	...	...	...	781,530	1,983,313	1,859,821
21. Cropland harvested, acres[16, 53]	...	...	...	...	...	...	...	...	...
22. Percentage increase in farm population[17, 18]	...	...	...	...	...	...	...	107.5	11.3
23. Percentage increase in number of farms[16, 17]	...	...	...	...	...	...	...	119.6	26.7
24. Percentage increase of land in farms[16, 17]	...	...	...	...	...	...	...	268.5	-20.6
25. Percentage increase of improved land in farms[17]	...	...	...	...	...	...	...	153.8	-6.2

General Population, Agriculture, and Manufacturing Statistics, 1790-1970

ARKANSAS

1880	1890	1900	1910	1920	1930	1940	1950	1960	1970
802,525	1,128,211	1,311,564	1,574,449	1,752,204	1,854,482	1,949,387	1,909,511	1,786,272	1,923,295
65.6	40.6	16.3	20.0	11.3	5.8	5.1	-2.0	-6.5	7.7
318,054	325,654	183,385	262,885	177,755	102,278	94,905	-39,876	-123,239	137,023
1.6	1.8	1.7	1.7	1.7	1.5	1.5	1.3	1.0	. . .
15.3	21.5	25.0	30.0	33.4	35.3	37.0	36.3	34.0	37.0
5	6	7	7	7	7	7	6	4	4
591,531	818,752	944,580	1,131,026	1,279,757	1,375,315	1,466,084	1,481,507	1,395,703	1,565,915
63.4	38.4	15.4	19.7	13.1	7.5	6.6	1.0	-5.8	12.2
210,666	309,117	366,856	442,891	472,220	478,463	482,578	426,639	388,787	352,445
72.4	46.7	18.7	20.7	6.6	1.3	0.9	-11.6	-8.9	-9.4
. . .	. . .	. . .	. . .	. . .	. . .	. . .	. . .	. . .	. . .
32,020	73,159	111,733	202,681	290,497	382,878	431,910	617,153[c] 630,591[d]	742,869[c] 765,303[d]	960,865
158.6	128.5	52.7	81.4	43.3	31.8	12.8	42.9[c] . . .[d]	20.4[c] 21.4[d]	25.6
770,505	1,055,052	1,199,831	1,371,768	1,461,707	1,471,604	1,517,477	1,292,358[c] 1,278,920[d]	1,043,403[c] 1,020,969[d]	962,430
63.2	36.9	13.7	14.3	6.6	0.7	3.1	-14.8[c] . . .[d]	-19.3[c] -20.2[d]	-5.7
4.0	6.5	8.5	12.9	16.6	20.6	22.2	32.3[c] 33.0[d]	41.6[c] 42.8[d]	50.0
96.0	93.5	91.5	87.1	83.4	79.4	77.8	67.7[c] 67.0[d]	58.4[c] 57.2[d]	50.0
94,433	124,760	178,694	214,678	232,604	242,334	216,674	182,429	95,007[e]	74,000
12,061,547	14,891,356	16,636,719	17,416,075	17,456,750	16,052,962	18,044,542	18,871,244	16,458,515[e]	17,900,000
3,595,603	5,475,043	6,953,735	8,076,254	9,210,556	. . .	. . .	. . .	. . .	. . .
2,755,901	3,982,999	5,017,894	5,376,484	6,465,305	6,581,834	6,609,833	5,930,093	5,324,541[e]	7,342,000
65.6	40.6	16.3	20.0	11.3	-2.4	. . .	. . .	. . .	. . .
91.1	32.1	43.2	20.1	8.4	4.2	-10.6	-15.8	-47.9[e]	. . .
58.8	23.5	11.7	4.7	0.2	-8.0	12.4	4.6	-12.8[e]	. . .
93.3	52.3	27.0	16.1	14.0	. . .	. . .	. . .	. . .	. . .

Item No.	1790 (or 1789)	1800	1810	1820	1830	1840	1850	1860	1870*
26. Average acreage per farm[16]	...	...	...	...	...	...	146.3	245.4	153.7
27. Percentage increase in cropland harvested[16]	...	...	...	...	...	...	...	...	...
28. Value of farms, dollars[16]	...	...	...	...	...	...	15,265,245	91,649,773	32,023,758
29. Value of farms, percent increase[16]	...	...	...	...	...	...	...	500.4	-65.1
30. Average value per farm, dollars[16]	...	...	...	...	...	...	860	2,350	648
31. Farms operated by owners[19, 20, 21, 22, 23, 24]	...	...	...	...	...	...	...	...	...
32. Value of livestock on farms, dollars[25, 26, 27, 54]	...	...	...	...	...	...	6,647,969	22,096,977	13,778,005[h]
33. Average value of livestock per farm, dollars[25, 26, 27, 52, 54]	...	...	...	...	...	...	374	567	279[h]
34. Production of cotton in commercial bales[28, 29, 30, 31, 53]	...	...	...	...	...	...	65,344	367,393	247,968
35. Percent of total production of cotton[28, 29, 30, 31, 53]	...	...	...	...	...	...	2.6	6.8	8.2
36. Production of corn in bushels[32, 33, 34, 35, 53]	...	...	...	...	...	...	8,893,939	17,823,588	13,382,145
37. Percent of total production of corn[32, 33, 34, 35, 53]	...	...	...	...	...	...	1.5	2.1	1.8
38. Production of tobacco in pounds[36, 37, 38]	...	...	...	...	...	...	218,936	989,980	594,886
39. Percent of total production of tobacco[36, 37, 38]	...	...	...	...	...	...	0.1	0.2	0.2
40. Production of rice in pounds[39, 53]	...	...	...	...	...	...	63,179	16,831	73,021
41. Production of rice in bushels[40, 41]	...	...	...	...	...	...	...	...	...
42. Percent of total production of rice[39, 40, 41, 53]	...	...	...	...	...	...	...	...	0.1
43. Number of manufacturing establishments[42, 43, 44, 45, 46, 55]	...	...	...	...	...	...	261	518	1,079
44. Capital of manufacturing establishments[42, 43, 44]	...	...	...	...	...	...	305,015	1,316,610	1,782,913
45. Average number of wages earners[42, 43, 44, 45, 46, 55]	...	...	...	...	...	...	842	1,877	3,206
46. Total wages[42, 43, 45, 46, 55]	...	...	...	...	...	...	159,876	554,240	673,963
47. Cost of materials used in manufacturing[42, 43, 44, 45, 46, 55]	...	...	...	...	...	...	215,789	1,280,503	2,536,998
48. Value of manufactured product[42, 43, 44, 45, 46]	...	...	...	...	...	...	537,908	2,880,578	4,629,234

a. Census corrected by reference to counties constituting present state area.

b. Reported as for "settlements of Hope Field and St. Francis" and for "settlements on the Arkansas" in the unorganized territory then called "Louisiana Territory."

c. Previous urban definition. Rural included population residing outside of incorporated places having 2,500 inhabitants or more.

d. Current urban definition. Urban includes those residing in urban-fringe areas and in unincorporated places of 2,500 or more.

e. For 1959.

f. Based on a sampling of farms

g. Includes part owners

h. Values in gold

i. Computed on data available

j. For 1967

k. Less than .1%

*The 1870 Census of population is considered incomplete in the Southern states.

General Population, Agriculture, and Manufacturing Statistics, 1790-1970—ARKANSAS (Cont.)

1880	1890	1900	1910	1920	1930	1940	1950	1960	1970
127.7	119.4	93.1	81.1	75.0	66.2	83.3	103.4	173.2[e]	...
...	44.5	26.0	7.1	20.3	1.8	0.4	-10.3	-10.2[e]	...
74,249,655	118,574,422	135,182,170	309,166,813	753,110,666	547,828,250	456,848,156	1,135,671,000[f]	1,797,070,000[e,f]	...
131.9	59.7	14.0	128.7	143.6	-27.2	-16.6	148.6[f]	58.2[e,f]	...
786	950	757	1,440	3,238	2,261	2,108	6,225[f]	18,915[e,f]	...
65,245	84,706	97,554	106,649[g]	112,647[g]	89,009[g]	100,636[g]	113,283[g]	72,044[e,g]	...
20,472,425	30,772,880	37,483,771	74,058,292	127,852,580	68,573,100	70,071,421	132,708,736	153,906,398[e]	271,225,000
217	247	210	345	550	283	323	727	1,620[e]	3,665
608,256	619,494	709,880	776,879	869,350	1,398,475	1,351,209	1,584,307	1,484,003	1,048,000
10.6	9.3	7.5	7.3	7.6	9.6	11.8	10.3	10.7[i]	10.3
24,156,417	33,982,318	44,144,098	37,609,544	34,226,935	27,388,105	33,762,323	21,626,026	14,945,000	1,575,000
1.4	1.6	1.7	1.5	1.4	1.3	1.5	0.8	0.3	**[k]
970,220	954,790	831,700	316,418	267,050	94,750	81,731	34,103	23,024	...
0.2	0.2	...	...	...	...	...	...	...	...
...	7,110	8,630	...	...	...	...	...	...	...
...	...	...	1,282,830	6,797,126	6,958,105	7,651,231	19,889,614	28,143,014	2,102,400,000
...	...	...	5.6	18.9	20.7	17.4	22.2[i]	23.3[i]	25.1
1,202	2,073	4,794	2,925	3,123	1,731	1,178)			2,911[j]
2,953,130	14,971,614	35,960,640	70,174,000	138,818,000	...	...)			...
4,557	14,143	26,501	44,982	49,954	44,205	36,256)			143,600[j]
925,358	4,649,186	8,686,291	19,113,000	47,186,000	39,503,000	24,577,000)	See following table		656,600,000[j]
4,392,080	12,397,261	23,963,768	34,935,000	102,813,000	116,648,000	92,777,000)			2,354,200,000[j]
6,756,159	22,659,179	45,197,731	74,916,000	200,313,000	210,903,000	160,167,000)			...

General Population, Agriculture, and Manufacturing Statistics, 1790–1970

DELAWARE

Item No.	1790 (or 1789)	1800	1810	1820	1830	1840	1850	1860	1870*
1. Population[1,50]	59,096	64,273	72,674	72,749	76,748	78,085	91,532	112,216	125,015
2. Decennial rates of increase in population over preceding census[2,50]	...	8.8	13.1	0.1	5.5	1.7	17.2	22.6	11.4
3. Increase in population over previous census[1,3,50]	...	5,177	8,401	75	3,999	1,337	13,447	20,684	12,799
4. Percent distribution of population[4]	1.5	1.2	1.0	0.8	0.6	0.5	0.4	0.4	0.3
5. Population per square mile of land area[5,6,50]	...	32.7	...	...	...	...	46.6	57.1	63.6
6. Membership of House of Representatives at each apportionment[7]	1	1	2	1	1	1	1	1	1
7. White population[8,9,10,51]	46,310	49,852	55,361	55,282	57,601	58,561	71,169	90,589	102,221
8. Percentage increase in white population over preceding census[9,10,11,51]	...	7.6	11.1	-0.1	4.2	1.7	21.5	27.3	12.8
9. Negro population[8,9,10,51]	12,786	14,421	17,313	17,467	19,147	19,524	20,363	21,627	22,794
10. Percentage increase in Negro population over preceding census[9,10,11,12,13,51]	...	12.8	20.1	0.9	9.6	2.0	4.3	6.2	5.4
11. Number of slaves in the area enumerated in 1790 and in the added area[14]	8,887	6,153	4,177	4,509	3,292	2,605	2,290	1,798	...
12. Urban population[15,50]	...	...	...	...	...	8,367	13,979	21,258	30,841
13. Percent urban increase over preceding census[15,50]	...	...	...	...	...	...	67.1	52.1	45.1
14. Rural population[15,50]	59,096	64,273	72,674	72,749	76,748	69,718	77,553	90,958	94,174
15. Percent rural increase over preceding census[15,50]	...	8.8	13.1	0.1	5.5	-9.2	11.2	17.3	3.5
16. Percent of urban to total population[15,50]	...	...	...	...	...	10.7	15.3	18.9	24.7
17. Percent of rural to total population[15,50]	100.0	100.0	100.0	100.0	100.0	89.3	84.7	81.1	75.3
18. Number of farms[16,52]	...	...	...	...	...	...	6,063	6,658	7,615
19. Acres in farms[16,52]	...	...	...	...	...	...	956,144	1,004,295	1,052,322
20. Acres improved land in farms[17]	...	...	...	...	...	...	580,862	637,065	698,115
21. Cropland harvested, acres[16,53]	...	...	...	...	...	...	...	...	...
22. Percentage increase in farm population[17,18]	...	...	...	...	...	...	...	22.6	11.4
23. Percentage increase in number of farms[16,17]	...	...	...	...	...	...	...	9.8	14.4
24. Percentage increase of land in farms[16,17]	...	...	...	...	...	...	...	5.0	4.8
25. Percentage increase of improved land in farms[17]	...	...	...	...	...	...	...	9.7	9.6

General Population, Agriculture, and Manufacturing Statistics, 1790–1970

DELAWARE

1880	1890	1900	1910	1920	1930	1940	1950	1960	1970
146,608	168,493	184,735	202,322	223,003	238,380	266,505	318,085	446,292	548,104
17.3	14.9	9.6	9.5	10.2	6.9	11.8	19.4	40.3	22.8
21,593	21,885	16,242	17,587	20,681	15,377	28,125	51,580	128,207	101,812
0.3	0.3	0.2	0.2	0.2	0.2	0.2	0.2	0.2	...
74.6	85.7	94.0	103.0	113.5	120.5	134.7	160.8	225.6	276.5
1	1	1	1	1	1	1	1	1	1
120,160	140,066	153,977	171,102	192,615	205,718	230,528	273,878	384,327	466,459
17.5	16.6	9.9	11.1	12.6	6.8	12.1	18.9	40.3	21.4
26,442	28,386	30,697	31,181	30,335	32,602	35,876	43,598	60,688	78,276
16.0	7.4	8.1	1.6	-2.7	7.5	10.0	21.5	16.3	29.0
...	...	...	...	...	...	...	...	...	...
48,989	71,067	85,717	97,085	120,767	123,146	139,432	147,890[a] 199,122[b]	145,469[a] 292,788[b]	395,569
58.8	45.1	20.6	13.3	24.4	2.0	13.2	6.1[a] ...[b]	-1.6[a] 47.0[b]	35.1
97,619	97,426	99,018	105,237	102,236	115,234	127,073	170,195[a] 118,963[b]	300,823[a] 153,504[b]	152,535
3.7	-0.2	1.6	6.3	-2.9	12.7	10.3	33.9[a] ...[b]	76.8[a] 29.0[b]	-0.6
33.4	42.2	46.4	48.0	54.2	51.7	52.3	46.5[a] 62.6[b]	32.6[a] 65.6[b]	72.2
66.6	57.8	53.6	52.0	45.8	48.3	47.7	53.5[a] 37.4[b]	67.4[a] 34.4[b]	27.8
8,749	9,381	9,687	10,836	10,140	9,707	8,994	7,448	5,208[c]	3,700
1,090,245	1,055,692	1,066,228	1,038,866	944,511	900,815	895,507	851,291	762,526[c]	700,000
746,958	762,655	754,010	713,538	653,052	...	...	...	...	...
353,170	373,011	437,168	438,522	448,422	407,609	378,448	389,283	416,197[c]	491,000
17.3	14.9	9.6	9.5	10.2	-9.1	...	...	...	...
14.9	7.2	3.3	11.9	-6.4	-4.3	-7.3	-17.2	-30.1[c]	...
3.6	-3.2	1.0	-2.6	-9.1	-4.6	-0.6	-4.9	-10.4[c]	...
7.0	2.1	-1.1	-5.4	-8.5	...	...	...	...	...

11

Item No.	1790 (or 1789)	1800	1810	1820	1830	1840	1850	1860	1870*
26. Average acreage per farm[16]	...	...	...	...	...	...	157.7	150.8	138.2
27. Percentage increase in cropland harvested[16]	...	...	...	...	...	...	...	...	...
28. Value of farms, dollars[16]	...	...	...	...	...	...	18,880,031	31,426,357	37,370,296
29. Value of farms, percent increase[16]	...	...	...	...	...	...	...	66.5	18.9
30. Average value per farm, dollars[16]	...	...	...	...	...	...	3,114	4,720	4,907
31. Farms operated by owners[19, 20, 21, 22, 23, 24]	...	...	...	...	...	...	...	...	...
32. Value of livestock on farms, dollars[25, 26, 27, 54]	...	...	...	...	...	...	1,849,281	3,144,706	3,405,858[f]
33. Average value of livestock per farm, dollars,[25, 26, 27, 52, 54]	...	...	...	...	...	...	305	472	447[f]
34. Production of cotton in commercial bales[28, 29, 30, 31]	...	...	...	...	...	...	...	...	...
35. Percent of total production of cotton[28, 29, 30, 31]	...	...	...	...	...	...	...	...	...
36. Production of corn in bushels[32, 33, 34, 35, 53]	...	...	...	...	...	...	3,145,542	3,892,337	3,010,390
37. Percent of total production of corn[32, 33, 34, 35, 53]	...	...	...	...	...	...	0.5	0.5	0.4
38. Production of tobacco in pounds[36, 37, 38]	...	...	...	...	...	...	...	9,699	250
39. Percent of total production of tobacco[36, 37, 38]	...	...	...	...	...	...	...	...	...
40. Production of rice in pounds[39]	...	...	...	...	...	...	...	...	...
41. Production of rice in bushels[40, 41]	...	...	...	...	...	...	...	...	...
42. Percent of total production of rice[39, 40, 41]	...	...	...	...	...	...	...	...	...
43. Number of manufacturing establishments[42, 43, 44, 45, 46, 55]	...	...	...	...	...	...	531	615	800
44. Capital of manufacturing establishments[42, 43, 44]	...	...	...	...	...	...	2,978,945	5,452,887	10,839,093
45. Average number of wage earners[42, 43, 44, 45, 46, 55]	...	...	...	...	...	...	3,888	6,421	9,710
46. Total wages[42, 43, 45, 46, 55]	...	...	...	...	...	...	936,924	1,905,754	3,692,195
47. Cost of materials used in manufacturing[42, 43, 44, 45, 46, 55]	...	...	...	...	...	...	2,864,607	6,028,918	10,206,397
48. Value of manufactured product[42, 43, 44, 45, 46]	...	...	...	...	...	...	4,649,296	9,892,902	16,791,382

a. Previous urban/rural definition. Rural included population residing outside of incorporated places having 2,500 inhabitants or more.
b. Current urban/rural definition. Urban includes those residing in urban-fringe areas and in unincorporated places of 2,500 or more.
c. For 1959
d. Based on a sampling of farms
e. Includes part owners
f. Value in gold
g. Based on data available
h. For 1967

*The 1870 Census of population is considered incomplete in the Southern states

General Population, Agriculture, and Manufacturing Statistics, 1790-1970—Delaware (Cont.)

1880	1890	1900	1910	1920	1930	1940	1950	1960	1970
124.6	112.5	110.1	95.9	93.1	92.8	99.6	114.3	146.4[c]	...
...	5.6	17.2	0.3	2.3	-9.1	-7.1	2.9	6.9[c]	...
36,789,672	39,586,080	34,436,040	53,155,983	64,755,631	66,941,747	54,898,828	97,141,000[d]	179,943,000[c, d]	...
-1.6	7.6	-13.0	54.4	21.8	3.4	-18.0	76.9[d]	85.2[c, d]	...
4,205	4,220	3,555	4,905	6,386	6,896	6,104	13,043[d]	34,551[c, d]	...
5,041	4,978	4,811	6,178[e]	6,010[e]	6,260[e]	5,956[e]	6,111[e]	4,453[c, e]	...
3,420,080	4,198,810	4,111,054	6,817,123	8,600,665	9,031,037	5,861,253	9,865,410	9,904,430[c]	8,818,000
391	448	424	629	848	930	652	1,325	1,902[c]	2,384
...	...	...	...	...	...	...	...	...	...
...	...	...	...	...	...	...	...	...	...
3,894,264	3,097,164	4,736,580	4,839,548	3,686,109	3,466,565	3,597,583	4,159,065	8,586,000	13,690,000
0.2	0.1	0.2	0.2	0.1	0.2	0.1	0.1	0.2	0.3
1,278	29,680	2,000	...	1,777	...	...	...	...	...
...	...	...	...	...	...	...	...	...	...
...	...	...	...	...	...	...	...	...	...
...	...	...	...	...	...	...	...	...	...
...	...	...	...	...	...	...	...	...	...
746	1,003	1,417	726	668	460	429)			528[h]
15,655,822	33,695,400	41,203,239	60,906,000	148,208,000	...	...)			...
12,638	20,479	22,203	21,238	29,035	23,552	20,392)	See following table		70,700[h]
4,267,349	8,630,475	9,259,661	10,296,000	37,265,000	29,063,000	21,960,000)			588,400,000[h]
12,828,461	21,161,752	26,652,601	30,938,000	85,433,000	80,491,000	59,570,000)			1,520,800,000[h]
20,514,438	37,571,848	45,387,630	52,840,000	165,073,000	149,642,000	114,754,000)			...

General Population, Agriculture, and Manufacturing Statistics, 1790–1970

FLORIDA

Item No.	1790 (or 1789)	1800	1810	1820	1830	1840	1850	1860	1870*
1. Population[1, 50]	...	...	...	...	34,730	54,477	87,445	140,424	187,748
2. Decennial rates of increase in population over preceding census[2, 50]	...	...	...	...	...	56.9	60.5	60.6	33.7
3. Increase in population over previous census[1, 3, 50]	...	...	...	...	34,730	19,747	32,968	52,979	47,324
4. Percent distribution of population[4]	...	...	...	...	0.3	0.3	0.4	0.4	0.5
5. Population per square mile of land area[5, 6, 50]	...	...	...	...	...	...	1.6	2.6	3.4
6. Membership of House of Representatives at each apportionment[7]	...	...	...	...	...	1	1	1	2
7. White population[8, 9, 10, 51]	...	...	...	...	18,385	27,943	47,203	77,746	96,057
8. Percentage increase in white population over preceding census[9, 10, 11, 51]	...	...	...	...	...	52.0	68.9	64.7	23.6
9. Negro population[8, 9, 10, 51]	...	...	...	...	16,345	26,534	40,242	62,677	91,689
10. Percentage increase in Negro population over preceding census[9, 10, 11, 12, 13, 51]	...	...	...	...	...	62.3	51.7	55.8	46.3
11. Number of slaves in the area enumerated in 1790 and in the added area[14]	...	...	...	...	15,501	25,717	39,310	61,745	...
12. Urban population[15, 50]	...	...	...	...	...	...	...	5,708	15,275
13. Percent urban increase over preceding census[15, 50]	...	...	...	...	...	...	...	...	167.6
14. Rural population[15, 50]	...	...	...	...	34,730	54,477	87,445	134,716	172,473
15. Percent rural increase over preceding census[15, 50]	...	...	...	...	...	56.9	60.5	54.1	28.0
16. Percent of urban to total population[15, 50]	...	...	...	...	...	...	...	4.1	8.1
17. Percent of rural to total population[15, 50]	...	...	...	...	100.0	100.0	100.0	95.9	91.9
18. Number of farms[16, 52]	...	...	...	...	...	...	4,304	6,568	10,241
19. Acres in farms[16, 52]	...	...	...	...	...	...	1,595,289	2,920,228	2,373,541
20. Acres improved land in farms[17]	...	...	...	...	...	...	349,049	654,213	736,172
21. Cropland harvested, acres[16, 53]	...	...	...	...	...	...	...	...	...
22. Percentage increase in farm population[17, 18]	...	...	...	...	...	...	...	60.6	33.7
23. Percentage increase in number of farms[16, 17]	...	...	...	...	...	...	...	52.6	55.9
24. Percentage increase of land in farms[16, 17]	...	...	...	...	...	...	...	83.1	-18.7
25. Percentage increase of improved land in farms[17]	...	...	...	...	...	...	...	87.4	12.5

General Population, Agriculture, and Manufacturing Statistics, 1790–1970

FLORIDA

1880	1890	1900	1910	1920	1930	1940	1950	1960	1970
269,493	391,422	528,542	752,619	968,470	1,468,211	1,897,414	2,771,305	4,951,560	6,789,443
43.5	45.2	35.0	42.4	28.7	51.6	29.2	46.1	78.7	37.1
81,745	121,929	137,120	224,077	215,851	499,741	429,203	873,891	2,180,255	1,837,883
0.5	0.6	0.7	0.8	0.9	1.2	1.4	1.8	2.8	...
4.9	7.1	9.6	13.7	17.7	27.1	35.0	51.1	91.3	125.5
2	2	3	4	4	5	6	8	12	15
142,605	224,949	297,333	443,634	638,153	1,035,390	1,381,986	2,166,051	4,063,881	5,719,343
48.5	57.7	32.2	49.2	43.8	62.2	33.5	56.7	87.6	40.7
126,690	166,180	230,730	308,669	329,487	431,828	514,198	603,101	880,186	1,041,651
38.2	31.2	38.8	33.8	6.7	31.1	19.0	17.2	45.9	18.3
...	...	...	...	...	...	...	...	...	...
26,947	77,358	107,031	219,080	353,515	759,778	1,045,791	1,566,788[a] 1,813,890[b]	3,077,989[a] 3,661,383[b]	5,468,137
76.4	187.1	38.4	104.7	61.4	114.9	37.6	49.8[a] ...[b]	96.5[a] 101.9[b]	49.3
242,546	314,064	421,511	533,539	614,955	708,433	851,623	1,204,517[a] 957,415[b]	1,873,571[a] 1,290,177[b]	1,321,306
40.6	29.5	34.2	26.6	15.3	15.2	20.2	41.4[a] ...[b]	55.5[a] 34.8[b]	2.4
10.0	19.8	20.3	29.1	36.5	51.7	55.1	56.5[a] 65.5[b]	62.2[a] 73.9[b]	80.5
90.0	80.2	79.7	70.9	63.5	48.3	44.9	43.5[a] 34.5[b]	37.8[a] 26.1[b]	19.5
23,438	34,228	40,814	50,016	54,005	58,966	62,248	56,921	45,100[c]	34,000
3,297,324	3,674,486	4,363,891	5,253,538	6,046,691	5,026,617	8,337,708	16,527,536	15,236,521[c]	16,200,000
947,640	1,145,693	1,511,653	1,805,408	2,297,271	...	...	...	...	...
684,630	715,633	1,019,968	1,223,078	1,237,009	1,454,254	1,679,622	1,728,232	1,881,879[c]	1,525,000
43.5	45.2	35.0	42.4	28.7	-1.0	...	...	...	...
128.9	46.0	19.2	22.5	8.0	9.2	5.6	-8.5	-20.8[c]	...
38.9	11.4	18.8	20.4	15.1	-16.9	65.9	98.2	-7.8[c]	...
28.7	20.9	31.9	19.4	27.2	...	...	...	...	...

Item No.	1790 (or 1789)	1800	1810	1820	1830	1840	1850	1860	1870*
26. Average acreage per farm[16]	...	...	...	...	...	...	370.7	444.6	231.8
27. Percentage increase in cropland harvested[16]	...	...	...	...	...	...	...	...	...
28. Value of farms, dollars[16]	...	...	...	...	...	...	6,323,109	16,435,727	7,958,336
29. Value of farms, percent increase[16]	...	...	...	...	...	...	...	159.9	-51.6
30. Average value per farm, dollars[16]	...	...	...	...	...	...	1,469	2,502	777
31. Farms operated by owners[19, 20, 21, 22, 23, 24]	...	...	...	...	...	...	...	...	...
32. Value of livestock on farms, dollars[25, 26, 27, 54]	...	...	...	...	...	...	2,880,058	5,553,356	4,169,726[f]
33. Average value of livestock per farm, dollars[25, 26, 27, 52, 54]	...	...	...	...	...	...	669	846	407[f]
34. Production of cotton in commercial bales[28, 29, 30, 31, 53]	...	...	...	...	...	...	45,131	65,153	39,789
35. Percent of total production of cotton[28, 29, 30, 31, 53]	...	...	...	...	...	...	1.8	1.2	1.3
36. Production of corn in bushels[32, 33, 34, 35, 53]	...	...	...	...	...	...	1,996,809	2,834,391	2,225,056
37. Percent of total production of corn[32, 33, 34, 35, 53]	...	...	...	...	...	...	0.3	0.3	0.3
38. Production of tobacco in pounds[36, 37, 38, 53]	...	...	...	...	...	...	998,614	828,815	157,405
39. Percent of total production of tobacco[36, 37, 38, 53]	...	...	...	...	...	...	0.5	0.2	0.1
40. Production of rice in pounds[39]	...	...	...	...	...	...	1,075,090	223,704	401,687
41. Production of rice in bushels[40, 41]	...	...	...	...	...	...	...	...	...
42. Percent of total production of rice[39, 40, 41]	...	...	...	...	...	...	0.5	0.1	0.5
43. Number of manufacturing establishments[42, 43, 44, 45, 46, 55]	...	...	...	...	...	...	103	185	659
44. Capital of manufacturing establishments[42, 43, 44]	...	...	...	...	...	...	547,060	1,874,125	1,679,930
45. Average number of wage earners[42, 43, 44, 45, 46, 55]	...	...	...	...	...	...	991	2,454	2,749
46. Total wages[42, 43, 45, 46, 55]	...	...	...	...	...	...	199,452	619,840	989,592
47. Cost of materials used in manufacturing[42, 43, 44, 45, 46, 55]	...	...	...	...	...	...	220,611	874,506	2,330,873
48. Value of manufactured product[42, 43, 44, 45, 46]	...	...	...	...	...	...	668,335	2,447,969	4,685,403

a. Previous urban/rural definition. Rural included population residing outside of incorporated places having 2,500 inhabitants or more.
b. Current urban/rural definition. Urban includes those residing in urban-fringe areas and in unincorporated places of 2,500 or more.
c. For 1959
d. Based on a sampling of farms
e. Includes part owners
f. Values in gold
g. Including estimated value of range animals
h. Based on data available
i. For 1967.

*The 1870 Census of population is considered incomplete in the Southern states.

1880	1890	1900	1910	1920	1930	1940	1950	1960	1970
140.7	107.4	106.9	105.0	112.0	85.2	133.9	290.4	337.8[c]	...
...	4.5	42.5	19.9	1.1	17.6	15.5	2.9	8.9[c]	...
20,291,835	72,745,180	40,799,838	118,145,989	281,449,404	423,346,262	324,377,874	945,871,000[d]	3,317,285,000[c,d]	...
155.0	258.5	-43.9	189.6	138.2	50.4	-23.4	191.6[d]	250.7[c,d]	...
866	2,125	1,000	2,362	5,212	7,179	5,211	16,617[d]	73,554[c,d]	...
16,198	26,140	29,994	35,399[e]	38,487[e]	39,394[e]	44,935[e]	48,966[e]	41,282[c,e]	...
6,920,980[g]	7,142,980	11,166,016	20,591,187	35,015,439	23,474,662	26,929,375	101,673,014	172,470,807[c]	303,317,000
295	209	274	412	654	398	433	1,786	3,824[c]	8,921
54,997	57,928	61,856	65,056	19,538	34,426	11,424	17,502	13,665	7,400
1.0	0.8	0.7	0.6	0.2	0.2	...	0.1[h]	0.1[h]	0.1
3,174,234	3,701,264	5,311,050	7,023,767	8,831,112	6,617,724	5,190,717	3,845,324	16,281,000	8,050,000
0.2	0.2	0.2	0.3	0.4	0.3	0.2	0.1	0.4	0.2
21,182	470,443	1,125,600	3,505,801	4,473,696	9,248,190	20,321,564	22,536,359	23,412,585	28,923,000
...	0.1	0.1	0.3	0.3	0.6	1.2	1.3	1.4	1.6
1,294,677	1,011,805	2,254,492	...	...	...	...	...	...	...
...	...	...	12,341	39,157	4,878	2,556	...	...	...
1.2	0.8	0.8	...	0.1	...	...	...	...	...
426	805	2,056	2,159	2,582	2,212	2,083)			7,950[i]
3,210,680	11,110,304	33,107,477	65,291,000	206,294,000	...	...)			...
5,504	13,119	34,230	57,473	74,415	64,868	52,732)	See following table		285,100[i]
1,270,875	5,918,614	10,683,038	22,982,000	67,433,000	54,582,000	37,883,000)			1,754,700,000[i]
3,040,119	8,021,854	15,637,520	26,128,000	92,680,000	96,898,000	123,523,000)			3,704,100,000[i]
5,546,448	18,222,890	36,810,243	72,890,000	213,327,000	232,386,000	241,539,000)			...

General Population, Agriculture, and Manufacturing Statistics, 1790—1970

GEORGIA

Item No.	1790 (or 1789)	1800	1810	1820	1830	1840	1850	1860	1870*
1. Population[1, 50]	82,548	162,686	252,433	340,989	516,823	691,392	906,185	1,057,286	1,184,109
2. Decennial rates of increase in population over preceding census[2, 50]	...	97.1	55.2	35.1	51.6	33.8	31.1	16.7	12.0
3. Increase in population over previous census[1, 3, 50]	...	80,138	89,747	88,556	175,834	174,569	214,793	151,101	126,823
4. Percent distribution of population[4]	2.1	3.1	3.5	3.5	4.0	4.1	3.9	3.4	3.1
5. Population per square mile of land area[5, 6, 50]	...	1.5	...	...	...	...	15.4	18.0	20.2
6. Membership of House of Representatives at each apportionment[7]	2[a]	4	6	7	9	8	8	7	9
7. White population[8, 9, 10, 51]	52,886	102,261	145,414	189,570	296,806	407,695	521,572	591,550	638,926
8. Percentage increase in white population over preceding census[9, 10, 11, 51]	...	93.4	42.2	30.4	56.6	37.4	27.9	13.4	8.0
9. Negro population[8, 9, 10, 51]	29,662	60,425	107,019	151,419	220,017	283,697	384,613	465,698	545,142
10. Percentage increase in Negro population over preceding census[9, 10, 11, 12, 13, 51]	...	10.4	77.1	41.5	45.3	28.9	35.6	21.1	17.1
11. Number of slaves in the area enumerated in 1790 and in the added area[14]	29,264	59,406	105,218	149,656	217,531	280,944	381,682	462,198	...
12. Urban population[15, 50]	...	5,146	5,215	7,523	14,013	24,658	38,994	75,466	100,053
13. Percent urban increase over preceding census[15, 50]	...	...	1.3	44.3	86.3	76.0	58.1	93.5	32.6
14. Rural population[15, 50]	82,548	157,540	247,218	333,466	502,810	666,734	867,191	981,820	1,084,056
15. Percent rural increase over preceding census[15, 50]	...	90.8	56.9	34.9	50.8	32.6	30.1	13.2	10.4
16. Percent of urban to total population[15, 50]	...	3.2	2.1	2.2	2.7	3.6	4.3	7.1	8.4
17. Percent of rural to total population[15, 50]	100.0	96.8	97.9	97.8	97.3	96.4	95.7	92.9	91.6
18. Number of farms[16, 52]	...	...	...	...	...	...	51,759	62,003	69,956
19. Acres in farms[16, 52]	...	...	...	...	...	...	22,821,379	26,650,490	23,647,941
20. Acres improved land in farms[17]	...	...	...	...	...	...	6,378,479	8,062,758	6,831,856
21. Cropland harvested, acres[16, 53]	...	...	...	...	...	...	...	...	...
22. Percentage increase in farm population[17, 18]	...	...	...	...	...	...	...	16.7	12.0
23. Percentage increase in number of farms[16, 17]	...	...	...	...	...	...	...	19.8	12.8
24. Percentage increase of land in farms[16, 17]	...	...	...	...	...	...	...	16.8	-11.3
25. Percentage increase of improved land in farms[17]	...	...	...	...	...	...	...	26.4	-15.3

General Population, Agriculture, and Manufacturing Statistics, 1790–1970

GEORGIA

1880	1890	1900	1910	1920	1930	1940	1950	1960	1970
1,542,180	1,837,353	2,216,331	2,609,121	2,895,832	2,908,506	3,123,723	3,444,578	3,943,116	4,589,575
30.2	19.1	20.6	17.7	11.0	0.4	7.4	10.3	14.5	16.4
358,071	295,173	378,978	392,790	286,711	12,674	215,217	320,855	498,538	646,459
3.1	2.9	2.9	2.8	2.7	2.4	2.4	2.3	2.2	...
26.3	31.3	37.7	44.4	49.3	49.7	53.4	58.9	67.7	79.0
10	11	11	12	12	10	10	10	10	10
816,906	978,357	1,181,294	1,431,802	1,689,114	1,837,021	2,038,278	2,380,577	2,817,223	3,391,242
27.9	19.8	20.7	21.2	18.0	8.7	10.9	16.8	18.3	20.4
725,133	858,815	1,034,813	1,176,987	1,206,365	1,071,125	1,084,927	1,062,762	1,122,596	1,187,149
33.0	18.4	20.5	13.7	2.5	-11.2	1.3	-2.0	5.6	5.8
...	...	...	...	...	...	...	...	...	...
145,090	257,472	346,382	538,650	727,859	895,492	1,073,808	1,426,206[b] 1,559,447[c]	1,963,012[b] 2,180,236[c]	2,768,074
45.0	77.5	34.5	55.5	35.1	23.0	19.9	32.8[b] ...[c]	37.6[b] 39.8[c]	27.0
1,397,090	1,579,881	1,869,949	2,070,471	2,167,973	2,013,014	2,049,915	2,018,372[b] 1,885,131[c]	1,980,104[b] 1,762,880[c]	1,821,501
28.9	13.1	18.4	10.7	4.7	-7.1	1.8	-1.5[b] ...[c]	-1.9[b] -6.5[c]	3.3
9.4	14.0	15.6	20.6	25.1	30.8	34.4	41.4[b] 45.3[c]	49.8[b] 55.3[c]	60.3
90.6	86.0	84.4	79.4	74.9	69.2	65.6	58.6[b] 54.7[c]	50.2[b] 44.7[c]	39.7
138,626	171,071	224,691	291,027	310,732	255,598	216,033	198,191	106,350[d]	77,000
26,043,282	25,200,435	26,392,057	26,953,413	25,441,061	22,078,630	23,683,631	25,751,055	19,657,615[d]	17,300,000
8,204,720	9,582,866	10,615,644	12,298,017	13,055,209	...	...	...	...	...
6,400,009	6,917,305	8,267,290	9,662,383	10,470,079	8,337,145	8,802,593	7,098,147	4,917,975[d]	3,900,000
30.2	19.1	20.6	17.7	11.0	-15.8	...	...	...	...
98.2	23.4	31.3	29.5	6.8	-17.7	-15.5	-8.2	-46.3[d]	...
10.1	-3.2	4.7	2.1	-5.6	-13.2	7.3	8.7	-23.7[d]	...
20.1	16.8	10.8	15.8	6.2	...	...	...	...	...

General Population, Agriculture, and Manufacturing Statistics, 1790-1970—GEORGIA (Cont.)

Item No.	1790 (or 1789)	1800	1810	1820	1830	1840	1850	1860	1870*
26. Average acreage per farm[16]	...	...	...	...	...	...	440.9	429.8	338.0
27. Percentage increase in cropland harvested[16]	...	...	...	...	...	...	...	...	...
28. Value of farms, dollars[16]	...	...	...	...	...	...	95,753,445	157,072,803	75,647,574
29. Value of farms, percent increase[16]	...	...	...	...	...	...	...	64.0	-51.8
30. Average value per farm, dollars[16]	...	...	...	...	...	...	1,850	2,533	1,081
31. Farms operated by owners[19, 20, 21, 22, 23, 24]	...	...	...	...	...	...	...	...	...
32. Value of livestock on farms, dollars[25, 26, 27, 54]	...	...	...	...	...	...	25,728,416	38,372,734	24,125,054[g]
33. Average value of livestock per farm, dollars[25, 26, 27, 52, 54]	...	...	...	...	...	...	497	619	345[g]
34. Production of cotton in commercial bales[28, 29, 30, 31, 53]	...	...	...	...	...	...	499,091	701,840	473,934
35. Percent of total production of cotton[28, 29, 30, 31, 53]	...	...	...	...	...	...	20.2	13.0	15.7
36. Production of corn in bushels[32, 33, 34, 35, 53]	...	...	...	...	...	...	30,080,099	30,776,293	17,646,459
37. Percent of total production of corn[32, 33, 34, 35, 53]	...	...	...	...	...	...	5.1	3.7	2.3
38. Production of tobacco in pounds[36, 37, 38, 53]	...	...	...	...	...	...	423,924	919,318	288,596
39. Percent of total production of tobacco[36, 37, 38, 53]	...	...	...	...	...	...	0.2	0.2	0.1
40. Production of rice in pounds[39]	...	...	...	...	...	...	38,950,691	52,507,652	22,277,380
41. Production of rice in bushels[40, 41]	...	...	...	...	...	...	...	...	...
42. Percent of total production of rice[39, 40, 41]	...	...	...	...	...	...	18.1	28.1	30.3
43. Number of manufacturing establishments[42, 43, 44, 45, 46, 55]	...	...	...	...	...	...	1,522	1,890	3,836
44. Capital of manufacturing establishments[42, 43, 44]	...	...	...	...	...	...	5,456,483	10,890,875	13,930,125
45. Average number of wage earners[42, 43, 44, 45, 46, 55]	...	...	...	...	...	...	8,368	11,575	17,871
46. Total wages[42, 43, 45, 46, 55]	...	...	...	...	...	...	1,709,664	2,925,148	4,844,508
47. Cost of materials used in manufacturing[42, 43, 44, 45, 46, 55]	...	...	...	...	...	...	3,404,917	9,986,532	18,583,731
48. Value of manufactured product[42, 43, 44, 45, 46]	...	...	...	...	...	...	7,082,075	16,925,564	31,196,115

a. Membership of House of Representatives in 1789: 3.
b. Previous urban/rural definition. Rural included population residing outside of incorporated places having 2,500 inhabitants or more.
c. Current urban/rural definition. Urban includes those residing in urban-fringe areas and in unincorporated places of 2,500 or more.
d. For 1959
e. Based on a sampling of farms
f. Includes part owners
g. Values in gold
h. Based on data available
i. For 1967

*The 1870 Census of population is considered incomplete in the Southern states.

General Population, Agriculture, and Manufacturing Statistics, 1790-1970—GEORGIA (Cont.)

1880	1890	1900	1910	1920	1930	1940	1950	1960	1970
187.9	147.3	117.5	92.6	81.9	86.4	109.6	129.9	184.8[d]	...
...	8.1	19.5	16.9	8.4	-20.4	5.6	-1.9	-30.7[d]	...
111,910,540	152,006,230	183,370,120	479,204,332	1,138,298,627	577,338,409	480,344,531	1,114,506,000[e]	1,908,362,000[d, e]	...
47.9	35.8	20.6	161.3	137.5	-49.3	-16.8	132.0[e]	71.2[d, e]	...
807	889	816	1,647	3,663	2,259	2,223	5,623[e]	17,944[d, e]	...
76,451	79,477	90,131	98,628[f]	102,123[f]	79,802[f]	85,181[f]	112,527[f]	79,883[d, f]	...
25,930,352	31,477,990	35,200,507	80,393,993	154,390,507	74,573,493	81,791,694	143,680,254	181,936,798[d]	321,503,000
187	184	157	276	499	292	379	725	1,711[d]	4,175
814,441	1,191,846	1,287,992	1,992,408	1,681,907	1,344,488	905,088	609,967	521,374	292,000
14.1	15.9	13.5	18.7	14.8	9.2	7.9	3.9	3.7[h]	2.9
23,202,018	29,261,422	34,032,230	39,374,569	51,492,033	39,492,897	37,603,790	37,837,343	81,909,000	44,206,000
1.3	1.4	1.3	1.5	2.2	1.8	1.6	1.4	1.9	1.1
228,590	263,752	1,105,600	1,485,994	10,584,968	82,363,722	94,408,855	102,504,527	98,307,505	133,305,000
0.1	0.1	0.1	0.1	0.8	5.6	5.5	5.8	6.0	7.0
25,369,687	14,556,432	¹1,174,562	...	...	...	...	...	...	...
...	...	...	148,698	59,711	18,292	2,196	...	...	...
23.0	11.3	3.9	0.6	0.2	...	...	...	...	...
3,593	4,285	7,504	4,792	4,803	4,179	3,150)			6,976[i]
20,672,410	56,921,580	89,789,656	202,778,000	448,700,000	...	...)			...
24,875	52,298	83,842	104,588	123,441	158,774	157,804)			423,100[i]
5,266,152	14,623,996	20,290,071	34,805,000	101,180,000	110,435,000	108,083,000 ·)	See following table		2,231,200,000[i]
24,143,939	35,774,480	58,232,202	116,970,000	440,490,000	427,805,000	394,087,000)			7,054,600,000[i]
36,440,948	68,917,020	106,654,527	202,863,000	693,237,000	722,454,000	677,403,000)			...

General Population, Agriculture, and Manufacturing Statistics, 1790-1970

KENTUCKY

Item No.	1790 (or 1789)	1800	1810	1820	1830	1840	1850	1860	1870*
1. Population[1, 50]	73,677	220,955	406,511	564,317	687,917	779,828	982,405	1,155,684	1,321,011
2. Decennial rates of increase in population over preceding census[2, 50]	. . .	199.9	84.0	38.8	21.9	13.4	26.0	17.6	14.3
3. Increase in population over previous census[1, 3, 50]	. . .	147,278	185,556	157,806	123,600	91,911	202,577	173,279	165,327
4. Percent distribution of population[4]	1.9	4.2	5.6	5.9	5.3	4.6	4.2	3.7	3.4
5. Population per square mile of land area[5, 6, 50]	. . .	5.5	. . .	. . .	. . .	. . .	24.4	28.8	32.9
6. Membership of House Representatives at each apportionment[7]	2	6	10	12	13	10	10	9	10
7. White population[8, 9, 10, 51]	61,133	179,873	324,237	434,826	517,787	590,253	761,413	919,484	1,098,692
8. Percentage increase in white population over preceding census[9, 10, 11, 51]	. . .	194.2	80.3	34.1	19.1	14.0	29.0	20.8	19.5
9. Negro population[8, 9, 10, 51]	12,544	41,082	82,274	129,491	170,130	189,575	220,992	236,167	222,210
10. Percentage increase in Negro population over preceding census[9, 10, 11, 12, 13, 51]	. . .	227.5	100.3	57.4	31.4	11.4	16.6	6.9	-5.9
11. Number of slaves in the area enumerated in 1790 and in the added area[14]	12,430	40,343	80,561	126,732	165,213	182,258	210,981	225,483	. . .
12. Urban population[15, 50]	. . .	. . .	4,326	9,291	16,367	30,948	73,804	120,624	195,896
13. Percent urban increase over preceding census[15, 50]	. . .	. . .	. . .	114.8	76.2	89.1	138.5	63.4	62.4
14. Rural population[15, 50]	73,677	220,955	402,185	555,026	671,550	748,880	908,601	1,035,060	1,125,115
15. Percent rural increase over preceding census[15, 50]	. . .	199.9	82.0	38.0	21.0	11.5	21.3	13.9	8.7
16. Percent of urban to total population[15, 50]	. . .	. . .	1.1	1.6	2.4	4.0	7.5	10.4	14.8
17. Percent of rural to total population[15, 50]	100.0	100.0	98.9	98.4	97.6	96.0	92.5	89.6	85.2
18. Number of farms[16, 52]	. . .	. . .	. . .	. . .	. . .	. . .	74,777	90,814	118,422
19. Acres in farms[16, 52]	. . .	. . .	. . .	. . .	. . .	. . .	16,949,748	19,163,261	18,660,106
20. Acres improved land in farms[17]	. . .	. . .	. . .	. . .	. . .	. . .	5,968,270	7,644,208	8,103,850
21. Cropland harvested, acres[16, 53]	. . .	. . .	. . .	. . .	. . .	. . .	. . .	. . .	. . .
22. Percentage increase in farm population[17, 18]	. . .	. . .	. . .	. . .	. . .	. . .	. . .	17.6	14.3
23. Percentage increase in number of farms[16, 17]	. . .	. . .	. . .	. . .	. . .	. . .	. . .	21.4	30.4
24. Percentage increase of land in farms[16, 17]	. . .	. . .	. . .	. . .	. . .	. . .	. . .	13.1	-2.6
25. Percentage increase of improved land in farms[17]	. . .	. . .	. . .	. . .	. . .	. . .	. . .	28.1	6.0

General Population, Agriculture, and Manufacturing Statistics, 1790-1970

KENTUCKY

1880	1890	1900	1910	1920	1930	1940	1950	1960	1970
1,648,690	1,858,635	2,147,174	2,289,905	2,416,630	2,614,589	2,845,627	2,944,806	3,038,156	3,218,706
24.8	12.7	15.5	6.6	5.5	8.2	8.8	3.5	3.2	5.9
327,679	209,945	288,539	142,731	126,725	197,959	231,038	99,179	93,350	180,550
3.3	3.0	2.8	2.5	2.3	2.1	2.2	1.9	1.7	...
41.0	46.3	53.4	57.0	60.1	65.2	70.9	73.9	76.2	81.2
11	11	11	11	11	9	9	8	7	7
1,377,179	1,590,462	1,862,309	2,027,951	2,180,560	2,388,452	2,631,425	2,742,090	2,820,083	2,981,766
25.3	15.5	17.1	8.9	7.5	9.5	10.2	4.2	2.8	5.7
271,451	268,071	284,706	261,656	235,938	226,040	214,031	201,921	215,949	230,793
22.2	-1.2	6.2	-8.1	-9.8	-4.2	-5.3	-5.6	6.9	6.9
...	...	...	...	...	...	...	...	...	...
249,923	356,713	467,668	555,442	633,543	799,026	849,327	985,739[a] 1,084,070[b]	1,144,583[a] 1,353,215[b]	1,684,053
27.6	42.7	31.1	18.8	14.1	26.1	6.3	16.1[a] ...[b]	16.1[a] 24.8[b]	24.4
1,398,767	1,501,922	1,679,506	1,734,463	1,783,087	1,815,563	1,996,300	1,959,067[a] 1,860,736[b]	1,893,573[a] 1,684,941[b]	1,534,653
24.3	7.4	11.8	3.3	2.8	1.8	10.0	-1.9[a] ...[b]	-3.3[a] -9.4[b]	-8.9
15.2	19.2	21.8	24.3	26.2	30.6	29.8	33.5[a] 36.8[b]	37.7[a] 44.5[b]	52.3
84.8	80.8	78.2	75.7	73.8	69.4	70.2	66.5[a] 63.2[b]	62.3[a] 55.5[b]	47.7
166,453	179,264	234,667	259,185	270,626	246,499	252,894	218,476	150,986[c]	123,000
21,495,240	21,412,229	21,979,422	22,189,127	21,612,772	19,927,286	20,294,016	19,441,774	17,030,675[c]	16,800,000
10,731,683	11,818,882	13,741,968	14,354,471	13,975,746	...	...	...	...	...
5,245,337	5,616,453	6,349,926	6,046,819	6,300,850	5,330,821	5,271,623	5,053,682	4,012,962[c]	3,707,000
24.8	12.7	15.5	6.6	5.5	...	...	...	...	...
40.6	7.7	30.9	10.4	4.4	-8.9	2.6	-13.6	-30.9[c]	...
15.2	-0.4	2.6	1.0	-2.6	-7.8	1.8	-4.2	-12.4[c]	...
32.4	10.1	16.3	4.5	-2.6	...	...	...	...	...

General Population, Agriculture, and Manufacturing Statistics, 1790-1970—KENTUCKY (Cont.)

Item No.	1790 (or 1789)	1800	1810	1820	1830	1840	1850	1860	1870*
26. Average acreage per farm[16]	...	...	...	...	...	...	226.7	211.0	157.6
27. Percentage increase in cropland harvested[16]	...	...	...	...	...	...	...	...	...
28. Value of farms, dollars[16]	...	...	...	...	...	...	155,021,262	291,496,955	248,991,133
29. Value of farms, percent increase[16]	...	...	...	...	...	...	...	88.0	-14.6
30. Average value per farm, dollars[16]	...	...	...	...	...	...	2,073	3,210	2,103
31. Farms operated by owners[19, 20, 21, 22, 23, 24]	...	...	...	...	...	...	...	...	...
32. Value of livestock on farms, dollars[25, 26, 27, 54]	...	...	...	...	...	...	29,661,436	61,868,237	53,029,875[f]
33. Average value of livestock per farm, dollars[25, 26, 27, 52, 54]	...	...	...	...	...	...	397	681	448[f]
34. Production of cotton in commercial bales[28, 29, 30, 31, 53]	...	...	...	...	...	...	758	...	1,080
35. Percent of total production of cotton[28, 29, 30, 31, 53]	...	...	...	...	...	...	...	...	...
36. Production of corn in bushels[32, 33, 34, 35, 53]	...	...	...	...	...	...	58,672,591	64,043,633	50,091,006
37. Percent of total production of corn[32, 33, 34, 35, 53]	...	...	...	...	...	...	9.9	7.6	6.6
38. Production of tobacco in pounds[36, 37, 38, 53]	...	...	...	...	...	...	55,501,196	108,126,840	105,305,869
39. Percent of total production of tobacco[36, 37, 38, 53]	...	...	...	...	...	...	27.8	24.9	40.1
40. Production of rice in pounds[39]	...	...	...	...	...	...	5,688	...	...
41. Production of rice in bushels[40, 41]	...	...	...	...	...	...	...	...	...
42. Percent of total production of rice[39, 40, 41]	...	...	...	...	...	...	...	...	...
43. Number of manufacturing establishments[42, 43, 44, 45, 46, 55]	...	...	...	...	...	...	3,609	3,450	5,390
44. Capital of manufacturing establishments[42, 43, 44]	...	...	...	...	...	...	11,810,462	20,256,579	29,277,809
45. Average number of wage earners[42, 43, 44, 45, 46, 55]	...	...	...	...	...	...	21,476	21,258	30,636
46. Total wages[42, 43, 45, 46, 55]	...	...	...	...	...	...	5,106,048	6,020,082	9,444,524
47. Cost of materials used in manufacturing[42, 43, 44, 45, 46, 55]	...	...	...	...	...	...	12,165,075	22,295,759	29,497,535
48. Value of manufactured product[42, 43, 44, 45, 46]	...	...	...	...	...	...	21,710,212	37,931,240	54,625,809

a. Previous urban/rural definition. Rural included population residing outside of incorporated places having 2,500 inhabitants or more.
b. Current urban/rural definition. Urban includes those residing in urban-fringe areas and in unincorporated places of 2,500 or more.
c. For 1959
d. Based on a sampling of farms
e. Includes part owners
f. Values in gold
g. Based on data available
h. Less than .1%
i. For 1967

*The 1870 Census of population is considered incomplete in the Southern states.

1880	1890	1900	1910	1920	1930	1940	1950	1960	1970
129.1	119.4	93.7	85.6	79.9	80.8	80.2	89.0	112.8[c]	...
...	7.1	13.1	-4.8	4.2	15.4	-1.1	-4.1	-20.6[c]	...
299,298,631	346,339,360	382,004,890	635,459,372	1,305,158,936	871,448,632	776,494,098	1,572,256,000[d]	2,305,473,000[c, d]	...
20.2	15.7	10.3	66.3	105.4	-33.2	-10.9	102.4[d]	46.6[c, d]	...
1,798	1,932	1,628	2,452	4,823	3,535	3,070	7,196[d]	15,269[c, d]	...
122,426	134,529	157,602	170,332[e]	179,327[e]	157,403[e]	168,604[e]	168,948[e]	126,253[c, e]	...
49,670,567	70,924,400	73,739,106	117,486,662	157,191,298	120,931,359	103,422,377	257,415,282	306,353,207[c]	514,348,000
298	396	314	453	585	491	409	1,178	2,029[c]	4,182
1,367	873	1,369	3,469	2,967	8,955	15,704	12,887	10,653	2,400
...	...	...	...	...	0.1	0.1	0.1[g]	0.1[g]	**[h]
72,852,263	78,434,847	73,974,220	83,348,024	71,518,484	61,008,387	61,052,096	71,009,754	85,775,000	49,400,000
4.2	3.7	2.8	3.3	3.0	2.9	2.6	2.6	2.0	1.2
171,120,784	221,880,303	314,288,050	398,482,301	504,661,592	376,648,533	324,518,411	404,881,235	335,099,159	411,871,000
36.2	45.5	36.2	37.7	36.8	25.8	19.1	22.9	20.3	21.6
...	...	...	...	...	...	...	...	...	...
...	...	...	...	...	...	...	...	...	...
...	...	...	...	...	...	...	...	...	...
5,328	7,745	9,560	4,776	3,957	2,246	1,640)			2,994[i]
45,813,039	79,811,980	104,070,791	172,779,000	276,535,000	...	...)			...
37,391	56,558	62,962	65,400	69,340	77,825	62,794)	See following table		224,600[i]
11,657,844	21,326,831	22,434,185	27,888,000	67,034,000	88,644,000	61,902,000)			1,351,900,000[i]
47,461,890	63,677,583	82,830,415	111,779,000	235,716,000	266,559,000	293,629,000)			4,180,500,000[i]
75,483,377	126,719,851	154,166,365	223,754,000	395,660,000	502,639,000	481,030,000)			...

General Population, Agriculture, and Manufacturing Statistics, 1790-1970

LOUISIANA

Item No.	1790 (or 1789)	1800	1810	1820	1830	1840	1850	1860	1870*
1. Population[1, 50]	...	...	76,556	153,407	215,739	352,411	517,762	708,002	726,915
2. Decennial rates of increase in population over preceding census[2, 50]	...	...	...	100.4	40.6	63.4	46.9	36.7	2.7
3. Increase in population over previous census[1, 3, 50]	...	...	76,556	76,851	62,332	136,672	165,351	190,240	18,913
4. Percent distribution of population[4]	...	...	1.1	1.6	1.7	2.1	2.2	2.3	1.9
5. Population per square mile of land area[5, 6, 50]	...	...	...	...	...	...	11.4	15.6	16.0
6. Membership of House of Representatives at each apportionment[7]	...	...	1	3	3	4	4	5	6
7. White population[8, 9, 10, 51]	...	...	34,311[a]	73,867	89,441	158,457	255,491	357,456	362,065
8. Percentage increase in white population over preceding census[9, 10, 11, 51]	...	...	...	115.3	21.1	77.2	61.2	39.9	1.3
9. Negro population[8, 9, 10, 51]	...	...	42,245[a]	79,540	126,298	193,954	262,271	350,373	364,210
10. Percentage increase in Negro population over preceding census[9, 10, 11, 12, 13, 51]	...	...	...	88.3	58.8	53.6	35.2	33.6	3.9
11. Number of slaves in the area enumerated in 1790 and in the added area[14]	...	...	34,660[a]	69,064	109,588	168,452	244,809	331,726	...
12. Urban population[15, 50]	...	...	17,242	27,176	46,082	105,400	134,470	185,026	202,523
13. Percent urban increase over preceding census[15, 50]	...	...	...	57.6	69.6	128.7	27.6	37.6	9,5
14. Rural population[15, 50]	...	...	59,314	126,231	169,657	247,011	383,292	522,976	524,392
15. Percent rural increase over preceding census[15, 50]	...	...	...	112.8	34.4	45.6	55.2	36.4	0.3
16. Percent of urban to total population[15, 50]	...	...	22.5	17.7	21.4	29.9	26.0	26.1	27.9
17. Percent of rural to total population[15, 50]	...	...	77.5	82.3	78.6	70.1	74.0	73.9	72.1
18. Number of farms[16, 52]	...	...	...	...	...	...	13,422	17,328	28,481
19. Acres in farms[16, 52]	...	...	...	...	...	...	4,989,043	9,298,576	7,025,817
20. Acres improved land in farms[17]	...	...	...	...	...	...	1,590,025	2,707,108	2,045,640
21. Cropland harvested, acres[16, 53]	...	...	...	...	...	...	...	...	...
22. Percentage increase in farm population[17, 18]	...	...	...	...	...	...	...	36.7	2.7
23. Percentage increase in number of farms[16, 17]	...	...	...	...	...	...	...	29.1	64.4
24. Percentage increase of land in farms[16, 17]	...	...	...	...	...	...	...	86.4	-24.4
25. Percentage increase of improved land in farms[17]	...	...	...	...	...	...	...	70.3	-24.4

General Population, Agriculture, and Manufacturing Statistics, 1790-1970

LOUISIANA

1880	1890	1900	1910	1920	1930	1940	1950	1960	1970
939,946	1,118,588	1,381,625	1,656,388	1,798,509	2,101,593	2,363,880	2,683,516	3,257,022	3,641,306
29.3	19.0	23.5	19.9	8.6	16.9	12.5	13.5	21.4	11.8
213,031	178,641	263,038	274,763	142,121	303,084	262,287	319,636	573,506	384,284
1.9	1.8	1.8	1.8	1.7	1.7	1.8	1.8	1.8	...
20.7	24.6	30.4	36.5	39.6	46.5	52.3	59.4	72.2	81.0
6	6	7	8	8	8	8	8	8	8
454,954	558,395	729,612	941,086	1,096,611	1,322,712	1,511,739	1,796,683	2,211,715	2,541,498
25.7	22.7	30.7	29.0	16.5	20.6	14.2	18.8	23.1	14.9
483,655	559,193	650,804	713,874	700,257	776,326	849,303	882,428	1,039,207	1,086,832
32.8	15.6	16.4	9.7	-1.9	10.9	9.4	3.9	17.8	4.6
...	...	...	...	...	...	...	...	...	...
239,390	283,845	366,288	496,516	628,163	833,532	980,439	1,379,998[b] 1,471,696[c]	1,831,812[b] 2,060,606[c]	2,406,150
18.2	18.6	29.0	35.6	26.5	32.7	17.6	40.8[b] ...[c]	32.7[b] 40.0[c]	16.8
700,556	834,743	1,015,337	1,159,872	1,170,346	1,268,061	1,383,441	1,303,518[b] 1,211,820[c]	1,425,210[b] 1,196,416[c]	1,235,156
33.6	19.2	21.6	14.2	0.9	8.3	9.1	-5.8[b] ...[c]	9.3[b] -1.3[c]	3.2
25.5	25.4	26.5	30.0	34.9	39.7	41.5	51.4[b] 54.8[c]	56.2[b] 63.3[c]	66.1
74.5	74.6	73.5	70.0	65.1	60.3	58.5	48.6[b] 45.2[c]	43.8[b] 36.7[c]	33.9
48,292	69,294	115,969	120,546	135,463	161,445	150,007	124,181	74,438[d]	53,000
8,273,506	9,544,219	11,059,127	10,439,481	10,019,822	9,355,437	9,996,108	11,202,278	10,347,328[d]	12,200,000
2,739,972	3,774,668	4,666,532	5,276,016	5,626,226	...	...	...	...	...
1,913,360	2,477,134	3,408,944	3,586,348	3,924,267	4,068,151	4,051,670	3,148,881	2,425,936[d]	3,914,000
29.3	19.0	23.5	19.9	8.6	5.7	...	...	...	...
69.6	43.5	67.4	3.9	12.4	19.2	-7.1	-17.2	-40.0[d]	...
17.8	15.4	15.9	-5.6	-4.0	-6.6	6.8	12.1	-7.6[d]	...
33.9	37.8	23.6	13.1	6.6	...	...	...	...	...

General Population, Agriculture, and Manufacturing Statistics, 1790-1970—LOUISIANA (Cont.)

Item No.	1790 (or 1789)	1800	1810	1820	1830	1840	1850	1860	1870*
26. Average acreage per farm[16]	...	...	...	...	...	...	371.7	536.6	246.7
27. Percentage increase in cropland harvested[16]	...	...	...	...	...	...	...	...	...
28. Value of farms, dollars[16]	...	...	...	...	...	...	75,814,398	204,789,662	54,572,337
29. Value of farms, percent increase[16]	...	...	...	...	...	...	...	170.1	-73.4
30. Average value per farm, dollars[16]	...	...	...	...	...	...	5,649	11,818	1,916
31. Farms operated by owners[19, 20, 21, 22, 23, 24]	...	...	...	...	...	...	...	...	...
32. Value of livestock on farms, dollars[25, 26, 27, 54]	...	...	...	...	...	...	11,152,275	24,546,940	12,743,350[9]
33. Average value of livestock per farm, dollars[25, 26, 27, 52, 54]	...	...	...	...	...	...	831	1,417	447[9]
34. Production of cotton in commercial bales[28, 29, 30, 31, 53]	...	...	...	...	...	...	178,737	777,738	350,832
35. Percent of total production of cotton[28, 29, 30, 31, 53]	...	...	...	...	...	...	7.2	14.5	11.7
36. Production of corn in bushels[32, 33, 34, 35, 53]	...	...	...	...	...	...	10,266,373	16,853,745	7,596,628
37. Percent of total production of corn[32, 33, 34, 35, 53]	...	...	...	...	...	...	1.7	2.0	1.0
38. Production of tobacco in pounds[36, 37, 38, 53]	...	...	...	...	..	...	26,878	39,940	15,541
39. Percent of total production of tobacco[36, 37, 38, 53]	...	...	...	...	...	...	...	...	...
40. Production of rice in pounds[39, 53]	...	...	...	...	...	...	4,425,349	6,331,257	15,854,012
41. Production of rice in bushels[40, 41]	...	...	...	...	...	...	...	...	...
42. Percent of total production of rice[39, 40, 41, 53]	...	...	...	...	...	...	2.1	3.4	21.5
43. Number of manufacturing establishments[42, 43, 44, 45, 46, 55]	...	...	...	...	...	...	1,008	1,744	2,557
44. Capital of manufacturing establishments[42, 43, 44]	...	...	...	...	...	...	5,032,424	7,151,172	18,313,974
45. Average number of wage earners[42, 43, 44, 45, 46, 55]	...	...	...	...	...	...	6,217	8,789	30,071
46. Total wages[42, 43, 45, 46, 55]	...	...	...	...	...	...	2,033,928	3,683,679	4,593,470
47. Cost of materials used in manufacturing[42, 43, 44, 45, 46, 55]	...	...	...	...	...	...	2,459,508	6,738,486	12,412,023
48. Value of manufactured product[42, 43, 44, 45, 46]	...	...	...	...	...	...	6,779,417	15,587,473	24,161,905

a. In 1810 Louisiana was called "Orleans territory" and the name "Louisiana territory" was applied to the remainder of the Louisiana Purchase which was then unorganized.

b. Previous urban/rural definition. Rural included population residing outside of incorporated placed having 2,500 inhabitants or more.

c. Current urban/rural definition. Urban includes those residing in urban-fringe areas and in unincorporated places of 2,500 or more.

d. For 1959

e. Based on a sampling of farms

f. Includes part owners

g. Values in gold

h. Based on data available

i. Less than .1%

i. For 1967

*The 1870 Census of population is considered incomplete in the Southern states.

General Population, Agriculture, and Manufacturing Statistics, 1790-1970—LOUISIANA (Cont.)

1880	1890	1900	1910	1920	1930	1940	1950	1960	1970
171.3	137.7	95.4	86.6	74.0	57.9	66.6	90.2	139.0[d]	...
...	29.5	37.6	5.2	9.4	3.7	-0.4	-22.3	-22.9[d]	...
58,989,117	85,381,270	141,130,610	237,544,450	474,038,793	418,191,773	353,873,506	920,939,000	1,765,573,000[d, e]	...
8.1	44.7	65.3	68.3	99.6	-11.8	-15.4	160.2	91.7[d, e]	...
1,222	1,232	1,217	1,971	3,499	2,590	2,359	7,416	23,719[d, e]	...
31,286	38,539	48,735	52,989[f]	57,254[f]	53,159[f]	60,312[f]	74,394[f]	56,019[d, f]	...
12,345,905	17,898,380	28,869,506	43,314,683	82,634,450	55,320,377	60,646,142	147,861,044	197,452,676[d]	246,352,000
256	258	249	371	613	343	404	1,191	2,653[d]	4,648
508,569	659,180	709,041	268,909	306,791	798,828	717,713	607,186	479,298	521,000
8.8	8.8	7.4	2.5	2.7	5.5	6.2	3.9[h]	3.4[h]	5.1
9,889,689	13,081,954	22,062,580	26,010,361	21,675,602	18,279,702	22,444,412	13,030,057	17,490,000	4,998,000
0.6	0.6	0.8	1.0	0.9	0.8	1.0	0.5	0.4	0.1
55,954	46,845	102,100	172,418	221,277	81,047	374,383	256,794	73,660	189,000
...	...	...	...	...	...	...	...	...	**[i]
23,188,311	75,645,433	172,732,430	...	...	...	...	...	...	2,039,700,000
...	...	...	10,839,973	16,011,667	16,317,463	17,785,440	23,601,143	30,147,451	...
21.0	58.8	60.9	47.6	44.5	48.5	40.5	26.4[h]	24.9[h]	24.4
1,553	2,613	4,350	2,516	2,617	1,989	1,861)			3,639[j]
11,462,468	34,754,121	113,084,294	221,816,000	462,209,000	...	...)			...
12,167	28,377	42,210	76,165	98,265	87,345	71,218)			164,500[j]
4,360,371	10,122,569	15,385,715	33,386,000	94,406,000	83,867,000	55,084,000)	See following table		1,084,400,000[j]
14,442,506	33,282,724	82,299,893	134,865,000	431,404,000	438,540,000	365,179,000)			4,536,500,000[j]
24,205,183	57,806,713	121,181,683	223,949,000	676,189,000	685,037,000	565,265,000)			...

General Population, Agriculture, and Manufacturing Statistics, 1790-1970

MARYLAND

Item No.	1790 (or 1789)	1800	1810	1820	1830	1840	1850	1860	1870*
1. Population[1, 50]	319,728	341,548	380,546	407,350	447,040	470,019	583,034	687,049	780,894
2. Decennial rates of increase in population over preceding census[2, 50]	...	6.8	11.4	7.0	9.7	5.1	24.0	17.8	13.7
3. Increase in population over previous census[1, 3, 50]	...	21,820	38,998	26,804	39,690	22,979	113,015	104,015	93,845
4. Percent distribution of population[4]	8.1	6.4	5.3	4.2	3.5	2.8	2.5	2.2	2.0
5. Population per square mile of land area[5, 6, 50]	...	34.4	...	...	...	...	58.6	69.1	78.6
6. Membership of House of Representatives at each apportionment[7]	8[a]	9	9	9	8	6	6	5	6
7. White population[8, 9, 10, 51]	208,649	216,326	235,117	260,223	291,108	318,204	417,943	515,918	605,497
8. Percentage increase in white population over preceding census[9, 10, 11, 51]	...	3.7	8.7	10.7	11.9	9.3	31.3	23.4	17.4
9. Negro population[8, 9, 10, 51]	111,079	125,222	145,429	147,127	155,932	151,815	165,091	171,131	175,391
10. Percentage increase in Negro population over preceding census[9, 10, 11, 12, 13, 51]	...	12.7	16.1	1.2	6.0	-2.6	8.7	3.7	2.5
11. Number of slaves in the area enumerated in 1790 and in the added area[14, b]	103,036	107,707[c]	115,056[c]	111,917[c]	107,499[c]	93,057[c]	94,055	90,374	...
12. Urban population[15, 50]	13,503	26,514	46,555	66,378	91,041	113,912	188,045	233,300	295,459
13. Percent urban increase over preceding census[15, 50]	...	96.4	75.6	42.6	37.2	25.1	65.1	24.1	26.6
14. Rural population[15, 50]	306,225	315,034	333,991	340,972	355,999	356,107	394,989	453,749	485,435
15. Percent rural increase over preceding census[15, 50]	...	2.9	6.0	2.1	4.4	...	10.9	14.9	7.0
16. Percent of urban to total population[15, 50]	4.2	7.8	12.2	16.3	20.4	24.2	32.3	34.0	37.8
17. Percent of rural to total population[15, 50]	95.8	92.2	87.8	83.7	79.6	75.8	67.7	66.0	62.2
18. Number of farms[16, 52]	...	...	...	...	...	...	21,860	25,494	27,000
19. Acres in farms[16, 52]	...	...	...	...	...	...	4,634,350	4,835,571	4,512,579
20. Acres improved land in farms[17]	...	...	...	...	...	...	2,797,905	3,002,267	2,914,007
21. Cropland harvested, acres[16, 53]	...	...	...	...	...	...	...	...	...
22. Percentage increase in farm population[17, 18]	...	...	...	...	...	...	...	17.8	13.7
23. Percentage increase in number of farms[16, 17]	...	...	...	...	...	...	...	16.6	5.9
24. Percentage increase of land in farms[16, 17]	...	...	...	...	...	...	...	4.3	-6.7
25. Percentage increase of improved land in farms[17]	...	...	...	...	...	...	...	7.3	-2.9

General Population, Agriculture, and Manufacturing Statistics, 1790-1970

MARYLAND

1880	1890	1900	1910	1920	1930	1940	1950	1960	1970
934,943	1,042,390	1,188,044	1,295,346	1,449,661	1,631,526	1,821,244	2,343,001	3,100,689	3,922,399
19.7	11.5	14.0	9.0	11.9	12.5	11.6	28.6	32.3	26.5
154,049	107,447	145,654	107,302	154,315	181,865	189,718	521,757	757,688	821,710
1.9	1.7	1.6	1.4	1.4	1.3	1.4	1.5	1.7	...
94.0	104.9	119.5	130.3	145.8	165.0	184.2	237.1	314.0	396.6
6	6	6	6	6	6	6	7	8	8
724,693	826,493	952,424	1,062,639	1,204,737	1,354,226	1,518,481	1,954,975	2,573,919	3,194,888
19.7	14.0	15.2	11.6	13.4	12.4	12.1	28.7	31.6	24.1
210,230	215,657	235,064	232,250	244,479	276,379	301,931	385,972	518,410	699,479
19.9	2.6	9.0	-1.2	5.3	13.0	9.2	27.8	34.3	34.9
...	...	...	...	...	...	...	...	...	...
375,843	495,702	591,206	658,192	869,422	974,869	1,080,351	1,425,707[d] 1,615,902[e]	1,742,138[d] 2,253,832[e]	3,003,935
27.2	31.9	19.3	11.3	32.1	12.1	10.8	32.0[d] ...[e]	22.2[d] 39.5[e]	33.3
559,100	546,688	596,838	637,154	580,239	656,657	740,893	917,294[d] 727,099[e]	1,358,551[d] 846,857[e]	918,464
15.2	-2.2	9.2	6.8	-8.9	13.2	12.8	23.8[d] ...[e]	48.1[d] 16.5[e]	8.5
40.2	47.6	49.8	50.8	60.0	59.8	59.3	60.8[d] 69.0[e]	56.2[d] 72.7[e]	76.6
59.8	52.4	50.2	49.2	40.0	40.2	40.7	39.2[d] 31.0[e]	43.8[d] 27.3[e]	23.4
40,517	40,798	46,012	48,923	47,908	43,203	42,110	36,107	25,122[f]	18,300
5,119,831	4,952,390	5,170,075	5,057,140	4,757,999	4,374,398	4,197,827	4,055,529	3,456,769[f]	3,220,000
3,342,700	3,412,908	3,516,352	3,354,767	3,136,728	...	...	...	...	...
1,680,192	1,662,333	1,940,093	1,931,972	1,991,030	1,741,615	1,608,856	1,531,421	1,455,921[f]	1,446,000
19.7	11.5	14.0	9.0	11.9	15.0	...	...	...	...
50.1	0.7	12.8	6.3	-2.1	-9.8	-2.5	-14.2	-30.4[f]	...
13.5	-3.3	4.4	-2.2	-5.9	-8.1	-4.0	-3.4	-14.8[f]	...
14.7	2.1	3.0	-4.6	-6.5	...	...	...	...	...

Item No.	1790 (or 1789)	1800	1810	1820	1830	1840	1850	1860	1870*
26. Average acreage per farm[16]	...	...	...	...	...	...	212.0	189.7	167.1
27. Percentage increase in cropland harvested[16]	...	...	...	...	...	...	...	...	...
28. Value of farms, dollars[16]	...	...	...	...	...	...	87,178,545	145,973,677	136,295,747
29. Value of farms, percent increase[16]	...	...	...	...	...	...	...	67.4	-6.6
30. Average value per farm, dollars[16]	...	...	...	...	...	...	3,988	5,726	5,048
31. Farms operated by owners[19, 20, 21, 22, 23, 24]	...	...	...	...	...	...	...	...	...
32. Value of livestock on farms, dollars[25, 26, 27, 54]	...	...	...	...	...	...	7,997,634	14,667,853	14,746,958[i]
33. Average value of livestock per farm, dollars[25, 26, 27, 52, 54]	...	...	...	...	...	...	366	575	546[i]
34. Production of cotton in commercial bales[28, 29, 30, 31]	...	...	...	...	...	...	...	...	...
35. Percent of total production of cotton[28, 29, 30, 31]	...	...	...	...	...	...	...	...	...
36. Production of corn in bushels[32, 33, 34, 35, 53]	...	...	...	...	...	...	10,749,858	13,444,922	11,701,817
37. Percent of total production of corn[32, 33, 34, 35, 53]	...	...	...	...	...	...	1.8	1.6	1.5
38. Production of tobacco in pounds[36, 37, 38, 63]	...	...	...	...	...	...	21,407,497	38,410,965	15,785,339
39. Percent of total production of tobacco[36, 37, 38, 53]	...	...	...	...	...	...	10.7	8.9	6.0
40. Production of rice in pounds[39]	...	...	...	...	...	...	...	...	...
41. Production of rice in bushels[40, 41]	...	...	...	...	...	...	...	...	...
42. Percent of total production of rice[39, 40, 41]	...	...	...	...	...	...	...	...	...
43. Number of manufacturing establishments[42, 43, 44, 45, 46, 55]	...	...	...	...	...	...	3,725	3,083	5,812
44. Capital of manufacturing establishments[42, 43, 44]	...	...	...	...	...	...	14,934,450	23,230,608	36,438,729
45. Average number of wage earners[42, 43, 44, 45, 46, 55]	...	...	...	...	...	...	30,212	28,403	44,860
46. Total wages[42, 43, 45, 46, 55]	...	...	...	...	...	...	7,403,832	7,190,672	12,682,817
47. Cost of materials used in manufacturing[42, 43, 44, 45, 46, 55]	...	...	...	...	...	...	17,690,836	25,494,007	46,897,032
48. Value of manufactured product[42, 43, 44, 45, 46]	...	...	...	...	...	...	33,043,892	41,735,157	76,593,613

a. Membership of House of Representatives in 1789: 6.
b. Includes District of Columbia.
c. Alexandria County, which from 1800 to 1840, inclusive, formed a part of the District of Columbia is in this enumeration included with Virginia, for comparative purposes
d. Previous urban/rural definition. Rural included population residing outside of incorporated places having 2,500 inhabitants or more.
e. Current urban/rural definition. Urban includes those residing in urban-fringe areas and in unincorporated places of 2,500 or more.
f. For 1959.
g. Based on a sampling of farms
h. Includes part owners
i. Values in gold
j. Based on data available.
k. For 1967

*The 1870 Census of population is considered incomplete fn the Southern states.

General Population, Agriculture, and Manufacturing Statistics, 1790-1970—MARYLAND (Cont.)

1880	1890	1900	1910	1920	1930	1940	1950	1960	1970
126.4	121.4	112.4	103.4	99.3	101.3	99.7	112.3	137.6[f]	...
...	1.1	16.7	-0.4	3.1	-12.5	-7.6	-4.8	-4.9[f]	...
165,503,341	175,058,550	175,178,310	241,737,123	386,596,850	356,170,168	273,980,352	507,225,000[g]	982,152,000[f, g]	...
21.4	5.8	0.1	38.0	59.9	-7.9	-23.1	12.1[g]	93.6[f, g]	...
4,085	4,291	3,807	4,941	8,070	8,244	6,506	14,048[g]	39,095[f, g]	...
27,978	28,154	30,565	33,519[h]	32,805[h]	30,823[h]	30,458[h]	29,058[h]	20,916[h, f]	...
15,865,728	19,194,320	20,855,877	32,570,134	47,764,365	43,303,575	31,456,509	71,892,868	88,980,601[f]	105,168,000
392	470	454	666	1,003	1,002	747	1,991	3,542[f]	5,747
...	...	...	...	...	...	...	...	...	...
...	...	...	...	...	...	...	...	...	...
15,968,533	14,928,142	19,766,510	17,911,436	21,083,076	14,543,218	15,449,757	16,761,266	26,838,000	40,172,000
0.9	0.7	0.7	0.7	0.9	0.7	0.7	0.6	0.6	1.0
26,082,147	12,356,838	24,589,480	17,845,699	17,336,859	21,624,127	28,209,323	35,532,656	32,567,804	29,430,000
5.5	2.5	2.8	1.7	1.3	1.5	1.6	2.0	2.0	1.5
...	...	...	...	...	...	...	...	...	...
...	...	...	...	...	...	...	...	...	...
...	...	...	...	...	...	...	...	...	...
6,787	7,485	9,879	4,837	4,937	3,231	2,893)			3,401[k]
56,742,384	119,667,316	163,147,260	251,227,000	619,607,000	...	...)			...
74,945	97,808	108,325	107,921	140,342	131,099	141,643)			287,600[k]
18,904,965	34,441,414	38,748,551	45,436,000	147,867,000	148,835,000)	156,783,000	See following table		1,956,000,000[k]
66,937,846	92,059,390	144,397,680	199,049,000	549,347,000	696,986,000	604,505,000)			4,303,100,000[k]
106,780,563	171,842,593	242,552,990	315,669,000	873,945,000	1,119,082,000	1,027,354,000)			...

General Population, Agriculture, and Manufacturing Statistics, 1790-1970

MISSISSIPPI

Item No.	1790 (or 1789)	1800	1810	1820	1830	1840	1850	1860	1870*
1. Population[1, 50]	...	7,600[a]	31,306[a]	75,448	136,621	375,651	606,526	791,305	827,922
2. Decennial rates of increase in population over preceding census[2, 50]	...	...	311.9	141.0	81.1	175.0	61.5	30.5	4.6
3. Increase in population over previous census[1, 3, 50]	...	...	23,706	44,142	61,173	239,030	230,875	184,779	36,617
4. Percent distribution of population[4]	...	0.1	0.4	0.8	1.1	2.2	2.6	2.5	2.1
5. Population per square mile of land area[5, 6, 50]	...	0.3	...	...	...	...	13.1	17.1	17.9
6. Membership of House of Representatives at each apportionment[7]	...	...	1	1	2	4	5	5	6
7. White population[8, 9, 10, 51]	...	4,146[b]	16,602[b]	42,176	70,443	179,074	295,718	353,899	382,896
8. Percentage increase in white population over preceding census[9, 10, 11, 51]	...	...	300.0	154.0	67.0	154.2	65.1	19.7	8.2
9. Negro population[8, 9, 10, 51]	...	3,454[b]	14,704[b]	33,272	66,178	196,577	310,808	437,404	444,201
10. Percentage increase in Negro population over preceding census[9, 10, 11, 12, 13, 51]	...	...	325.6	126.2	98.9	197.0	58.1	40.7	1.6
11. Number of slaves in the area enumerated in 1790 and in the added area[14]	...	2,995[a]	14,523[a]	32,814	65,659	195,211	309,878	436,631	...
12. Urban population[15, 50]	...	...	...	...	2,789	3,612	10,723	20,689	33,255
13. Percent urban increase over preceding census[15, 50]	...	...	...	...	...	29.5	196.9	92.9	60.7
14. Rural population[15, 50]	...	7,600	31,306	75,448	133,832	372,039	595,803	770,616	794,667
15. Percent rural increase over preceding census[15, 50]	...	...	311.9	141.0	77.4	178.0	60.1	29.3	3.1
16. Percent of urban to total population[15, 50]	...	...	...	...	2.0	1.0	1.8	2.6	4.0
17. Percent of rural to total population[15, 50]	...	100.0	100.0	100.0	98.0	99.0	98.2	97.4	96.0
18. Number of farms[16, 52]	...	...	...	...	...	...	33,960	42,840	68,023
19. Acres in farms[16, 52]	...	...	...	...	...	...	10,490,419	15,839,684	13,121,113
20. Acres improved land in farms[17]	...	...	...	...	...	...	3,444,358	5,065,755	4,209,146
21. Cropland harvested, acres[16, 53]	...	...	...	...	...	...	...	...	...
22. Percentage increase in farm population[17, 18]	...	...	...	...	...	...	...	30.5	4.6
23. Percentage increase in number of farms[16, 17]	...	...	...	...	...	...	...	26.1	58.8
24. Percentage increase of land in farms[16, 17]	...	...	...	...	...	...	...	51.0	-17.2
25. Percentage increase of improved land in farms[17]	...	...	...	...	...	...	...	47.1	-16.9

General Population, Agriculture, and Manufacturing Statistics, 1790-1970

MISSISSIPPI

1880	1890	1900	1910	1920	1930	1940	1950	1960	1970
1,131,597	1,289,600	1,551,270	1,797,114	1,790,618	2,009,821	2,183,796	2,178,914	2,178,141	2,216,912
36.7	14.0	20.3	15.8	-0.4	12.2	8.7	-0.2	...	1.8
303,675	158,003	261,670	245,844	-6,496	219,203	173,975	-4,882	-773	38,771
2.3	2.0	2.0	1.9	1.7	1.6	1.7	1.4	1.2	...
24.4	27.8	33.5	38.8	38.6	42.4	46.1	46.1	46.1	46.9
7	7	8	8	8	7	7	6	5	5
479,398	544,851	641,200	786,111	853,962	998,077	1,106,327	1,188,632	1,257,546	1,393,283
25.2	13.7	17.7	22.6	8.6	16.9	10.8	7.4	5.8	10.8
650,291	742,559	907,630	1,009,487	935,184	1,009,718	1,074,578	986,494	915,743	815,770
46.4	14.2	22.2	11.2	-7.4	8.0	6.4	-8.2	-7.2	-10.9
...	...	...	...	...	...	...	...	...	...
34,581	69,966	120,035	207,311	240,121	338,850	432,882	601,772[c] 607,162[d]	787,731[c] 820,805[d]	986,642
4.0	102.3	71.6	72.7	15.8	41.1	27.8	39.0[c] ...[d]	30.9[c] 35.2[d]	20.2
1,097,016	1,219,634	1,431,235	1,589,803	1,550,497	1,670,971	1,750,914	1,577,142[c] 1,571,752[d]	1,390,410[c] 1,357,336[d]	1,230,270
38.0	11.2	17.3	11.1	-2.5	7.8	4.8	-9.9[c] ...[d]	-11.8[c] -13.6[d]	-9.4
3.1	5.4	7.7	11.5	13.4	16.9	19.8	27.6[c] 27.9[d]	36.2[c] 37.7[d]	44.5
96.9	94.6	92.3	88.5	86.6	83.1	80.2	72.4[c] 72.1[d]	63.8[c] 62.3[d]	55.5
101,772	144,318	220,803	274,382	272,101	312,663	291,092	251,383	138,142	95,000
15,855,462	17,572,547	18,240,736	18,557,533	18,196,979	17,332,195	19,156,058	20,710,770	18,630,263[e]	17,500,000
5,216,937	6,849,390	7,594,428	9,008,310	9,325,677	...	...	...	...	...
3,980,356	4,873,809	5,570,380	6,158,719	6,359,538	6,597,112	6,952,931	6,136,206	4,564,307[e]	4,899,000
36.7	14.0	20.3	15.8	-0.4	7.3	...	...	...	...
49.6	41.8	53.0	24.3	-0.8	14.9	-6.9	-13.6	-45.0[e]	...
20.8	10.8	3.8	1.7	-1.9	-4.8	10.5	8.1	-10.0[e]	...
23.9	31.3	10.9	18.6	3.5	...	...	...	...	...

Item No.	1790 (or 1789)	1800	1810	1820	1830	1840	1850	1860	1870*
26. Average acreage per farm[16]	...	...	...	...	...	...	308.9	369.7	192.9
27. Percentage increase in cropland harvested[16]	...	...	...	...	...	...	...	...	...
28. Value of farms, dollars[16]	...	...	...	...	...	...	54,738,634	190,760,367	65,373,261
29. Value of farms, percent increase[16]	...	...	...	...	...	...	...	248.5	-65.7
30. Average value per farm, dollars[16]	...	...	...	...	...	...	1,612	4,453	961
31. Farms operated by owners[19, 20, 21, 22, 23, 24]	...	...	...	...	...	...	...	...	...
32. Value of livestock on farms, dollars[25, 26, 27, 54]	...	...	...	...	...	...	19,403,662	41,891,692	23,952,190[h]
33. Average value of livestock per farm, dollars[25, 26, 27, 52, 54]	...	...	...	...	...	...	571	978	352[h]
34. Production of cotton in commercial bales[28, 29, 30, 31, 53]	...	...	...	...	...	...	484,292	1,202,507	564,938
35. Percent of total production of cotton[28, 29, 30, 31, 53]	...	...	...	...	...	...	19.6	22.3	18.8
36. Production of corn in bushels[32, 33, 34, 35, 53]	...	...	...	...	...	...	22,446,552	29,057,682	15,637,316
37. Percent of total production of corn[32, 33, 34, 35, 53]	...	...	...	...	...	...	3.8	3.5	2.1
38. Production of tobacco in pounds[36, 37, 38]	...	...	...	...	...	...	49.960	159,141	61,012
39. Percent of total production of tobacco[36, 37, 38]	...	...	...	...	...	...	...	...	...
40. Production of rice in pounds[39, 53]	...	...	...	...	...	...	2,719,856	809,082	374,627
41. Production of rice in bushels[40, 41]	...	...	...	...	...	...	...	...	...
42. Percent of total production of rice[39, 40, 41, 53]	...	...	...	...	...	...	1.3	0.4	0.5
43. Number of manufacturing establishments[42, 43, 44, 45, 46, 55]	...	...	...	...	...	...	947	976	1,731
44. Capital of manufacturing establishments[42, 43, 44]	...	...	...	...	...	...	1,815,820	4,384,492	4,501,714
45. Average number of wage earners[42, 43, 44, 45, 46, 55]	...	...	...	...	...	...	3,154	4,775	5,941
46. Total wages[42, 43, 45, 46, 55]	...	...	...	...	...	...	771,528	1,618,320	1,547,428
47. Cost of materials used in manufacturing[42, 43, 44, 45, 46, 55]	...	...	...	...	...	...	1,275,771	3,146,636	4,364,206
48. Value of manufactured product[42, 43, 44, 45, 46]	...	...	...	...	...	...	2,912,068	6,590,687	8,154,758

a. Population of those parts of present state included in Mississippi Territory as then constituted.
b. Census source corrected by reference to counties constituting present state area.
c. Previous urban/rural definition. Rural included population residing outside of incorporated places having 2,500 inhabitants or more.
d. Current urban/rural definition. Urban includes those residing in urban-fringe areas and in unincorporated places of 2,500 or more.
e. For 1959
f. Based on a sampling of farms
g. Includes part owners
h. Values in gold
i. Based on data available
j. For 1967

*The 1870 Census of population is considered incomplete in the Southern states.

1880	1890	1900	1910	1920	1930	1940	1950	1960	1970
155.8	121.8	82.6	67.6	66.9	55.4	65.8	82.4	134.9[e]	...
...	22.4	14.3	10.6	3.3	3.7	5.4	-11.7	-25.6[e]	...
92,844,915	127,423,157	152,007,000	334,162,289	789,896,778	568,322,065	474,986,062	1,147,791,000[f]	1,974,266,000[e,f]	...
42.0	37.2	19.3	119.8	136.4	-28.0	-16.4	141.6[f]	72.0[e,f]	...
912	883	688	1,218	2,903	1,818	1,632	4,566[f]	14,292[e,f]	...
57,214	68,058	82,951	92,066[g]	91,310[g]	86,047[g]	97,266[g]	120,729[g]	93,810[e,g]	...
24,285,717	33,936,435	42,657,222	75,247,033	134,244,557	82,711,344	83,197,684	173,935,645	227,838,994[e]	389,653,000
239	235	193	274	496	264	286	692	1,649[e]	4,102
963,111	1,154,725	1,313,798	1,127,156	957,527	1,875,108	1,533,092	1,496,902	1,560,581	1,600,000
16.7	15.5	13.8	10.6	8.4	12.9	13.3	9.7[i]	11.2[i]	15.7
21,340,800	26,148,144	38,789,920	28,428,667	38,095,228	34,935,657	36,034,812	37,933,711	42,501,000	6,944,000
1.2	1.2	1.5	1.1	1.6	1.6	1.5	1.4	1.0	0.2
414,663	62,111	62,760	18,600	725,577	4,603	16,741	...	3,105	...
0.1	...	...	...	0.5	...	...	...	...	...
1,718,951	676,746	739,222	...	...	...	...	...	...	224,400,000
...	...	...	4,836	18,141	924	594	...	2,679,361	...
1.6	0.5	0.3	...	...	...	...	...	2.2[i]	2.7
1,479	1,698	4,772	2,598	2,455	1,911	1,294)			2,761[j]
4,727,600	14,896,884	35,807,419	72,393,000	154,117,000	...	...)			...
5,827	14,465	26,418	50,384	57,560	52,086	46,359)			160,400[j]
1,192,645	4,191,754	7,471,886	18,768,000	51,256,000	42,208,000	27,437,000)	See following table		764,000,000[j]
4,667,183	10,064,897	21,692,092	36,926,000	96,678,000	113,592,000	101,475,000)			2,111,800,000[j]
7,518,302	18,705,834	40,431,386	80,555,000	197,747,000	220,918,000	174,937,000)			...

General Population, Agriculture, and Manufacturing Statistics, 1790-1970

NORTH CAROLINA

Item No.	1790 (or 1789)	1800	1810	1820	1830	1840	1850	1860	1870*
1. Population[1, 50]	393,751	478,103	555,500	638,829	737,987	753,419	869,039	992,622	1,071,361
2. Decennial rates of increase in population over preceding census[2, 50]	...	21.4	16.2	15.0	15.5	2.1	15.3	14.2	7.9
3. Increase in population over previous census[1, 3, 50]	...	84,352	77,397	83,329	99,158	15,432	115,620	123,583	78,739
4. Percent distribution of population[4]	10.0	9.0	7.7	6.6	5.7	4.4	3.7	3.2	2.8
5. Population per square mile of land area[5, 6, 50]	...	9.8	...	...	...	...	17.8	20.4	22.0
6. Membership of House of Representatives at each apportionment[7]	10[a]	12	13	13	13	9	8	7	8
7. White population[8, 9, 10, 51]	288,204	337,764	376,410	419,200	472,843	484,870	553,028	629,942	678,470
8. Percentage increase in white population over preceding census[9, 10, 11, 51]	...	17.2	11.4	11.4	12.8	2.5	14.1	13.9	7.7
9. Negro population[8, 9, 10, 51]	105,547	140,339	179,090	219,629	265,144	268,549	316,011	361,522	391,650
10. Percentage increase in Negro population over preceding census[9, 10, 11, 12, 13, 51]	...	33.0	27.6	22.6	20.7	1.3	17.7	14.4	8.3
11. Number of slaves in the area enumerated in 1790 and in the added area[14]	100,783	133,296	168,824	204,917	245,601	245,817	288,548	331,059	...
12. Urban population[15, 50]	...	...	...	12,502	10,455	13,310	21,109	24,554	36,218
13. Percent urban increase over preceding census[15, 50]	...	...	...	...	-16.4	27.3	58.6	16.3	47.5
14. Rural population[15, 50]	393,751	478,103	555,500	626,327	727,532	740,109	847,930	968,068	1,035,143
15. Percent rural increase over preceding census[15, 50]	...	21.4	16.2	12.8	16.2	1.7	14.6	14.2	6.9
16. Percent of urban to total population[15, 50]	...	...	...	2.0	1.4	1.8	2.4	2.5	3.4
17. Percent of rural to total population[15, 50]	100.0	100.0	100.0	98.0	98.6	98.2	97.6	97.5	96.6
18. Number of farms[16, 52]	...	...	...	...	...	...	56,963	75,203	93,565
19. Acres in farms[16, 52]	...	...	...	...	...	...	20,996,983	23,762,969	19,835,410
20. Acres improved land in farms[17]	...	...	...	...	...	...	5,453,975	6,517,284	5,258,742
21. Cropland harvested, acres[16, 53]	...	...	...	...	...	...	...	...	...
22. Percentage increase in farm population[17, 18]	...	...	...	...	...	...	...	14.2	7.9
23. Percentage increase in number of farms[16, 17]	...	...	...	...	...	...	...	32.0	24.4
24. Percentage increase of land in farms[16, 17]	...	...	...	...	...	...	...	13.2	-16.5
25. Percentage increase of improved land in farms[17]	...	...	...	...	...	...	...	19.5	-19.3

General Population, Agriculture, and Manufacturing Statistics, 1790-1970

NORTH CAROLINA

1880	1890	1900	1910	1920	1930	1940	1950	1960	1970
1,399,750	1,617,949	1,893,810	2,206,287	2,559,123	3,170,276	3,571,623	4,061,929	4,556,155	5,082,059
30.7	15.6	17.1	16.5	16.0	23.9	12.7	13.7	12.2	11.5
328,389	218,197	275,863	312,477	352,836	611,153	401,347	490,306	494,226	525,904
2.8	2.6	2.5	2.4	2.4	2.6	2.7	2.7	2.5	...
28.7	33.2	38.9	45.3	52.5	64.5	72.7	82.7	92.9	104.1
9	9	10	10	10	11	12	12	11	11
867,242	1,055,382	1,263,603	1,500,511	1,783,779	2,234,958	2,567,635	2,983,121	3,399,285	3,901,767
27.8	21.7	19.7	18.7	18.9	25.3	14.9	16.2	13.9	14.8
531,277	561,018	624,469	697,843	763,407	918,647	981,298	1,047,353	1,116,021	1,126,478
35.7	5.6	11.3	11.7	9.4	20.3	6.8	6.7	6.5	0.9
...	...	...	...	...	...	...	...	...	...
55,116	115,759	186,790	318,474	490,370	809,847	974,175	1,238,193[b] 1,368,101[c]	1,647,085[b] 1,801,921[c]	2,285,168
52.2	110.0	61.4	70.5	54.0	65.2	20.3	27.1[b] ...[c]	33.0[b] 31.7[c]	26.8
1,344,634	1,502,190	1,707,020	1,887,813	2,068,753	2,360,429	2,597,448	2,823,736[b] 2,693,828[c]	2,909,070[b] 2,754,234[c]	2,796,891
29.9	11.7	13.6	10.6	9.6	14.1	10.0	8.7[b] ...[c]	3.0[b] 2.2[c]	1.5
3.9	7.2	9.9	14.4	19.2	25.5	27.3	30.5[b] 33.7[c]	36.2[b] 39.5[c]	45.0
96.1	92.8	90.1	85.6	80.8	74.5	72.7	69.5[b] 66.3[c]	63.8[b] 60.5[c]	55.0
157,609	178,359	224,637	253,725	269,763	279,708	278,276	288,508	190,567[d]	158,000
22,363,558	22,651,896	22,749,356	22,439,129	20,021,736	18,055,103	18,845,338	19,317,937	15,887,724[d]	16,000,000
6,481,191	7,828,569	8,327,106	8,813,056	8,198,409	...	...	...	...	...
4,634,339	5,205,938	5,609,144	5,737,037	5,850,997	5,809,741	6,125,386	5,782,407	4,746,364[d]	4,123,000
30.7	15.6	17.1	16.5	16.0	6.6	...	...	...	...
68.4	13.2	25.9	12.9	6.3	3.7	-5.1	3.7	-33.9[d]	...
12.7	1.3	0.4	-1.4	-10.8	-9.8	4.4	2.5	-17.7[d]	...
23.2	20.8	6.4	5.8	-7.0	...	...	...	...	...

General Population, Agriculture, and Manufacturing Statistics, 1790-1970—NORTH CAROLINA (Cont.)

Item No.	1790 (or 1789)	1800	1810	1820	1830	1840	1850	1860	1870*
26. Average acreage per farm	...	...	...	...	...	...	368.6	316.0	212.0
27. Percentage increase in cropland harvested[16]	...	...	...	...	...	...	...	...	...
28. Value of farms, dollars[16]	...	...	...	...	...	...	67,891,766	143,301,065	62,568,866
29. Value of farms, percent increase[16]	...	...	...	...	...	...	...	111.1	-56.3
30. Average value per farm, dollars[16]	...	...	...	...	...	...	1,192	1,906	669
31. Farms operated by owners[19, 20, 21, 22, 23, 24]	...	...	...	...	...	...	...	...	...
32. Value of livestock on farms, dollars[25, 26, 27, 54]	...	...	...	...	...	...	17,717,647	31,130,805	17,595,174[9]
33. Average value of livestock per farm, dollars[25, 26, 27, 52, 54]	...	...	...	...	...	...	311	414	188[9]
34. Production of cotton in commercial bales[28, 29, 30, 31, 53]	...	...	...	...	...	...	73,845	145,514	144,935
35. Percent of total production of cotton[28, 29, 30, 31, 53]	...	...	...	...	...	...	3.0	2.7	4.8
36. Production of corn in bushels[32, 33, 34, 35, 53]	...	...	...	...	...	...	27,941,051	30,078,564	18,454,215
37. Percent of total production of corn[32, 33, 34, 35, 53]	...	...	...	...	...	...	4.7	3.6	2.4
38. Production of tobacco in pounds[36, 37, 38, 53]	...	...	...	...	...	...	11,984,786	32,853,250	11,150,087
39. Percent of total production of tobacco[36, 37, 38, 53]	...	...	...	...	...	...	6.0	7.6	4.2
40. Production of rice in pounds[39]	...	...	...	...	...	...	5,465,868	7,593,976	2,059,281
41. Production of rice in bushels[40, 41]	...	...	...	...	...	...	...	...	...
42. Percent of total production of rice[39, 40, 41]	...	...	...	...	...	...	2.5	4.1	2.8
43. Number of manufacturing establishments[42, 43, 44, 45, 46, 55]	...	...	...	...	...	...	2,663	3,689	3,642
44. Capital of manufacturing establishments[42, 43, 44]	...	...	...	...	...	...	7,456,860	9,693,703	8,140,473
45. Average number of wage earners[42, 43, 44, 45, 46, 55]	...	...	...	...	...	...	14,601	14,217	13,622
46. Total wages[42, 43, 45, 46, 55]	...	...	...	...	...	...	2,383,456	2,689,441	2,195,711
47. Cost of materials used in manufacturing[42, 43, 44, 45, 46, 55]	...	...	...	...	...	...	4,602,501	10,203,228	12,824,693
48. Value of manufactured product[42, 43, 44, 45, 46]	...	...	...	...	...	...	9,111,050	16,678,698	19,021,327

a. Membership of House of Representatives in 1789: 5.
b. Previous urban/rural definition. Rural included population residing outside of incorporated places having 2,500 inhabitants or more.
c. Current urban/rural definition. Urban includes those residing in urban-fringe areas and in unincorporated places of 2,500 or more.
d. For 1959
e. Based on a sampling of farms
f. Includes part owners
g. Values in gold
h. Based on data available
i. For 1967

*The 1870 Census of population is considered incomplete in the Southern states.

1880	1890	1900	1910	1920	1930	1940	1950	1960	1970
141.9	127.0	101.3	88.4	74.2	64.5	67.7	67.0	83.4[d]	...
...	12.3	7.7	2.3	2.0	-0.7	5.4	-5.6	-17.9[d]	...
135,793,602	183,977,010	194,655,920	456,624,607	1,076,392,960	844,121,809	736,708,125	1,905,714,000[e]	2,948,972,000[d,e]	...
117.0	35.5	5.8	134.6	135.7	-21.6	-12.7	158.6[e]	54.7[d,e]	...
862	1,031	867	1,800	3,990	3,018	2,647	6,605[e]	15,475[d,e]	...
104,887	117,469	131,629	145,320[f]	151,376[f]	141,445[f]	154,235[f]	177,507[f]	132,166[d,f]	...
22,414,659	25,547,280	30,106,173	62,649,984	118,254,961	78,537,148	89,925,652	146,286,671	155,842,492[d]	221,178,000
142	143	134	247	442	281	323	507	818[d]	1,400
389,598	336,261	459,707	665,132	858,406	764,328	458,146	472,389	318,638	155,000
6.8	4.5	4.8	6.2	7.5	5.2	4.0	3.1[h]	2.3[h]	1.5
28,019,839	25,783,623	34,818,860	34,063,531	40,998,317	35,608,833	50,797,461	58,054,020	85,914,000	70,000,000
1.6	1.2	1.3	1.3	1.7	1.7	2.2	2.1	2.0	1.7
26,986,213	36,375,258	127,503,400	138,813,163	280,163,432	454,222,610	715,616,397	661,981,561	654,438,670	815,520,000
5.7	7.5	14.7	13.1	20.4	31.2	42.1	37.4	39.7	42.7
5,609,191	5,846,404	7,892,580	...	...	...	...	...	...	...
...	...	...	...	...	...	...	...	...	...
5.1	4.6	2.8	...	...	...	...	...	...	...
3,802	3,667	7,226	4,931	5,999	3,797	3,225)			8,266[i]
13,045,639	32,745,995	76,503,894	217,185,000	669,144,000	...	...)			...
18,109	33,625	70,570	121,473	157,659	209,826	270,207)			643,800[i]
2,740,768	6,552,121	13,868,430	34,355,000	126,680,000	160,868,000	199,290,000)	See following table		3,066,100,000[i]
13,090,937	22,789,187	53,072,388	121,861,000	526,906,000	618,912,000	875,377,000)			8,592,800,000[i]
20,095,037	40,375,450	94,919,663	216,656,000	943,808,000	1,311,924,000	1,421,330,000)			...

OKLAHOMA

Item No.	1790 (or 1789)	1800	1810	1820	1830	1840	1850	1860	1870*
1. Population[1, 50]	...	...	...	...	...	...	...	...	...
2. Decennial rates of increase in population over preceding census[2, 50]	...	...	...	...	...	...	...	...	...
3. Increase in population over previous census[1, 3, 50]	...	...	...	...	...	...	...	...	...
4. Percent distribution of population[4]	...	...	...	...	...	...	...	...	...
5. Population per square mile of land area[5, 6, 50]	...	...	...	...	...	...	...	...	...
6. Membership of House of Representatives at each apportionment[7]	...	...	...	...	...	...	...	...	...
7. White population[8, 9, 10, 51]	...	...	...	...	...	...	...	...	...
8. Percentage increase in white population over preceding census[9, 10, 11, 51]	...	...	...	...	...	...	...	...	...
9. Negro population[8, 9, 10, 51]	...	...	...	...	...	...	...	...	...
10. Percentage increase in Negro population over preceding census[9, 10, 11, 12, 13, 51]	...	...	...	...	...	...	...	...	...
11. Number of slaves in the area enumerated in 1790 and in the added area[14]	...	...	...	...	...	...	...	...	...
12. Urban population[15, 50]	...	...	...	...	...	...	...	...	...
13. Percent urban increase over preceding census[15, 50]	...	...	...	...	...	...	...	...	...
14. Rural population[15, 50]	...	...	...	...	...	...	...	...	...
15. Percent rural increase over preceding census[15, 50]	...	...	...	...	...	...	...	...	...
16. Percent of urban to total population[15, 50]	...	...	...	...	...	...	...	...	...
17. Percent of rural to total population[15, 50]	...	...	...	...	...	...	...	...	...
18. Number of farms[16, 52]	...	...	...	...	...	...	...	...	...
19. Acres in farms[16, 52]	...	...	...	...	...	...	...	...	...
20. Acres improved land in farms[17]	...	...	...	...	...	...	...	...	...
21. Cropland harvested, acres[16, 53]	...	...	...	...	...	...	...	...	...
22. Percentage increase in farm population[17, 18]	...	...	...	...	...	...	...	...	...
23. Percentage increase in number of farms[16, 17]	...	...	...	...	...	...	...	...	...
24. Percentage increase of land in farms[16, 17]	...	...	...	...	...	...	...	...	...
25. Percentage increase of improved land in farms[17]	...	...	...	...	...	...	...	...	...
26. Average acreage per farm[16]	...	...	...	...	...	...	...	...	...

General Population, Agriculture, and Manufacturing Statistics, 1790-1970

OKLAHOMA

1880	1890	1900	1910	1920	1930	1940	1950	1960	1970
...	258,657	790,391	1,657,155	2,028,283	2,396,040	2,336,434	2,233,351	2,328,284	2,559,229
...	...	205.6	109.7	22.4	18.1	-2.5	-4.4	4.3	9.9
...	61,834	320,407[a]	866,764	371,128	367,757	-59,606	-103,103	94,933	230,945
...	0.4	1.0	1.8	1.9	1.9	1.8	1.5	1.3	
...	3.7[b]	11.4[b]	23.9	29.2	34.6	33.7	32.4	33.8	37.2
...	...	5	8	8	9	8	6	6	6
...	172,554[c]	670,204[c]	1,444,531	1,821,194	2,130,778	2,104,228	2,032,526	2,107,900	2,280,362
...	...	489.9[c]	115.5	26.1	17.0	-1.2	-3.4	3.7	8.2
...	21,609[c]	55,684[c]	137,612	149,408	172,198	168,849	145,503	153,084	171,892
...	...	533.4[c]	147.1	8.6	15.3	-1.9	-13.8	5.2	12.3
...	...	...	...	...	...	...	...	...	...
...	9,484	58,417	318,975	538,017	821,681	879,663	1,107,252[d] 1,139,481[e]	1,419,793[d] 1,464,786[e]	1,740,137
...	...	516.0	446.0	68.7	52.7	7.1	25.9[d] ...[e]	28.2[d] 28.5[e]	18.8
...	249,173	731,974	1,338,180	1,490,266	1,574,359	1,456,771	1,126,099[d] 1,093,870[e]	908,491[d] 863,498[e]	819,092
...	...	193.8	82.8	11.4	5.6	-7.5	-22.7[d] ...[e]	-19.3[d] -21.1[e]	-5.2
...	3.7	7.4	19.2	26.5	34.3	37.6	49.6[d] 51.0[e]	61.0[d] 62.9[e]	68.0
...	96.3	92.6	80.8	73.5	65.7	62.4	50.4[d] 49.0[e]	39.0[d] 37.1[e]	32.0
...	8,826[f]	108,000[g]	190,192	191,988	203,866	179,687	142,246	94,676[i]	91,000
...	1,606,423[f]	22,988,339[g]	28,859,353	31,951,934	33,790,817	34,803,317	36,006,603	35,800,688[i]	37,100,000
...	563,728[f]	8,574,187[g]	17,551,337	18,125,321	...	...	...	...	...
35,000[h]	122,932[h]	6,317,711[g]	11,921,670	15,132,769	15,553,185	12,766,219	11,896,040	8,975,117[i]	8,005,000
...	...	205.6[g]	109.7	22.4	0.7	...	...	...	...
...	...	[g,j]	76.1	0.9	6.2	-11.9	-20.8	-33.4[i]	...
...	...	[g,j]	25.5	10.7	5.7	3.0	3.4	-0.6[i]	...
...	...	...	104.7	3.3	...	...	...	...	...
...	182.0[f]	212.9[g]	151.7	166.4	165.8	193.7	253.1	378.1[i]	...

General Population, Agriculture, and Manufacturing Statistics, 1790-1970—OKLAHOMA (Cont.)

Item No.	1790 (or 1789)	1800	1810	1820	1830	1840	1850	1860	1870*
27. Percentage increase in cropland harvested[16]	...	...	...	...	...	...	...	...	...
28. Value of farms, dollars[16]	...	...	...	...	...	...	...	...	...
29. Value of farms, percent increase[16]	...	...	...	...	...	...	...	...	...
30. Average value per farm, dollars[16]	...	...	...	...	...	...	...	...	...
31. Farms operated by owners[19, 20, 21, 22, 23, 24]	...	...	...	...	...	...	...	...	...
32. Value of livestock on farms, dollars[25, 26, 27, 54]	...	...	...	...	...	...	...	...	...
33. Average value of livestock per farm, dollars[25, 26, 27, 52, 54]	...	...	...	...	...	...	...	...	...
34. Production of cotton in commercial bales[28, 29, 30, 31, 53]	...	...	...	...	...	...	...	...	...
35. Percent of total production of cotton[28, 29, 30, 31, 53]	...	...	...	...	...	...	...	...	...
36. Production of corn in bushels[32, 33, 34, 35, 53]	...	...	...	...	...	...	...	...	...
37. Percent of total production of corn[32, 33, 34, 35, 53]	...	...	...	...	...	...	...	...	...
38. Production of tobacco in pounds[36, 37, 38]	...	...	...	...	...	...	...	...	...
39. Percent of total production of tobacco[36, 37, 38]	...	...	...	...	...	...	...	...	...
40. Production of rice in pounds[39]	...	...	...	...	...	...	...	...	...
41. Production of rice in bushels[40, 41]	...	...	...	...	...	...	...	...	...
42. Percent of total production of rice[39, 40, 41]	...	...	...	...	...	...	...	...	...
43. Number of manufacturing establishments[42, 43, 44, 45, 46, 55]	...	...	...	...	...	...	...	...	...
44. Capital of manufacturing establishments[42, 43, 44]	...	...	...	...	...	...	...	...	...
45. Average number of wage earners[42, 43, 44, 45, 46, 55]	...	...	...	...	...	...	...	...	...
46. Total wages[42, 43, 45, 46, 55]	...	...	...	...	...	...	...	...	...
47. Cost of materials used in manufacturing[42, 43, 44, 45, 46, 55]	...	...	...	...	...	...	...	...	...
48. Value of manufactured product[42, 43, 44, 45, 46]	...	...	...	...	...	...	...	...	..

a. Exclusive of persons on Indian reservations.
b. Oklahoma and Indian Territory combined. Separate data are as follows: Indian Territory, 5.9 in 1890 and 12.7 in 1900; Oklahoma, 2.0 in 1890 and 10.3 in 1900.
c. Inlcudes Indian Territory in 1900 and, in 1890, persons specially enumerated in Indian Territory and on Indian reservations: Whites 117,368; Negroes, 18,636.
d. Previous urban/rural population definition. Rural included population residing outside of incorporated places having 2,500 inhabitants or more.
e. Current urban/rural population definition. Urban includes those residing in urban-fringe areas and in unincorporated places of 2,500 or more.
f. For Oklahoma Territory alone; excludes Indian Territory.
g. Includes Oklahoma Territory and Indian Territory.
h. Includes 35,078 acres of cotton in Indian Territory estimated from a special survey.
i. For 1959.
j. 1,000 percent or more
k. Based on a sampling of farms.
l. Includes part owners
m. Includes estimated value of range animals
n. Based on data available.
o. For 1967

General Population, Agriculture, and Manufacturing Statistics, 1790-1970—OKLAHOMA (Cont.)

1880	1890	1900	1910	1920	1930	1940	1950	1960	1970
...	251.2[h]	[g,j]	88.7	26.9	2.8	-17.9	-6.8	-24.5[i]	...
...	8,581,170[f]	170,804,675[g]	738,677,224	1,363,865,294	1,242,723,526	831,140,748	1,851,460,000	3,002,221,000[i,k]	...
...	...	[g,j]	332.5	84.6	-8.9	-33.1	2.4	62.1[i]	...
...	972[f]	1,582[g]	3,884	7,104	6,096	4,625	13,016	31,710[i]	...
...	8,761	49,346	85,404[l]	93,217[l]	77,714[l]	81,086[l]	97,038[l]	76,385[i,l]	...
876,000[m]	3,206,270	54,829,568	152,432,792	214,811,888	141,827,981	108,484,682	300,241,879	408,083,219[i]	812,887,000
...	363	877	801	1,125	696	604	2,111	4,310[i]	8,933
...	425	225,525[g]	555,742	1,006,242	1,130,415	520,591	567,792	364,833	193,000
...	...	2.3[g]	5.2	8.8	7.7	4.5	3.7	2.6[n]	1.9
...	234,315	68,949,300[g]	94,283,407	53,851,093	44,830,439	25,341,206	19,204,157	8,316,000	4,758,000
...	...	2.6[g]	3.7	2.3	2.1	1.1	0.7	0.2	0.1
...	...	108,910[g]	50,546	36,697	15,909	8,253	1,000	...	...
...	...	...	...	...	...	...	...	...	...
...	...	...	...	...	...	...	...	...	...
...	...	...	...	...	...	...	...	...	...
...	...	...	...	...	...	...	...	...	...
...	72	870	2,310	2,445	1,658	1,606)			2,611[o]
...	95,519	3,352,064	38,873,000	277,034,000	...	... 0			...
...	147	2,054	13,143	29,503	31,695	28,114)			117,700[o]
...	52,326	807,826	7,240,000	35,026,000	41,277,000	30,465,000)	See following table		764,200,000[o]
...	56,518	4,449,944	34,153,000	312,606,000	306,501,000	209,050,000)			1,962,700,000[o]
...	180,445	7,083,938	53,682,000	401,363,000	455,905,000	312,168,000)			...

General Population, Agriculture, and Manufacturing Statistics, 1790-1970

SOUTH CAROLINA

Item No.	1790 (or 1789)	1800	1810	1820	1830	1840	1850	1860	1870*
1. Population[1, 50]	249,073	345,591	415,115	502,741	581,185	594,398	668,507	703,708	705,606
2. Decennial rates of increase in population over preceding census[2, 50]	...	38.8	20.1	21.1	15.6	2.3	12.5	5.3	0.3
3. Increase in population over previous census[1, 3, 50]	...	96,518	69,524	87,626	78,444	13,213	74,109	35,201	1,898
4. Percent distribution of popualtion[4]	6.3	6.5	5.7	5.2	4.5	3.5	2.9	2.2	1.8
5. Population per square mile of land area[5, 6, 50]	...	11.3	...	...	...	...	21.9	23.1	23.1
6. Membership of House of Representatives at each apportionment[7]	6[a]	8	9	9	9	7	6	4	5
7. White population[8, 9, 10, 51]	140,178	196,255	214,196	237,440	257,863	259,084	274,563	291,300	289,667
8. Percentage increase in white population over preceding census[9, 10, 11, 51]	...	40.0	9.1	10.9	8.6	0.5	6.0	6.1	-0.6
9. Negro population[8, 9, 10, 51]	108,895	149,336	200,919	265,301	323,322	335,314	393,944	412,320	415,814
10. Percentage increase in Negro population over preceding census[9, 10, 11, 12, 13, 51]	...	37.1	34.5	32.0	21.9	3.7	17.5	4.7	0.8
11. Number of slaves in the area enumerated in 1790 and in the added area[14]	107,094	146,151	196,365	258,475	315,401	327,038	384,984	402,406	...
12. Urban population[15, 50]	16,359	18,824	24,711	24,780	33,599	33,601	49,045	48,574	61,011
13. Percent urban increase over preceding census[15, 50]	...	15.1	31.3	0.3	35.6	...	46.0	-1.0	25.6
14. Rural population[15, 50]	232,714	326,767	390,404	477,961	547,586	560,797	619,462	655,134	644,595
15. Percent rural increase over preceding census[15, 50]	...	40.4	19.5	22.4	14.6	2.4	10.5	5.8	-1.6
16. Percent of urban to total population[15, 50]	6.6	5.4	6.0	4.9	5.8	5.7	7.3	6.9	8.6
17. Percent of rural to total population[15, 50]	93.4	94.6	94.0	95.1	94.2	94.3	92.7	93.1	91.4
18. Number of farms[16, 52]	...	...	...	...	...	...	29,967	33,171	51,889
19. Acres in farms[16, 52]	...	...	...	...	...	...	16,217,700	16,195,919	12,105,280
20. Acres improved land in farms[17]	...	...	...	...	...	...	4,072,651	4,572,060	3,010,539
21. Cropland harvested, acres[16, 53]	...	...	...	...	...	...	...	...	...
22. Percentage increase in farm population[17, 18]	...	...	...	...	...	...	...	5.3	0.3
23. Percentage increase in number of farms[16, 17]	...	...	...	...	...	...	...	10.7	56.4
24. Percentage increase of land in farms[16, 17]	...	...	...	...	...	...	...	-0.1	-25.3
25. Percentage increase of improved land in farms[17]	...	...	...	...	...	...	...	12.3	-34.2

SOUTH CAROLINA

1880	1890	1900	1910	1920	1930	1940	1950	1960	1970
995,577	1,151,149	1,340,316	1,515,400	1,683,724	1,738,765	1,899,804	2,117,027	2,382,594	2,590,516
41.1	15.6	16.4	13.1	11.1	3.3	9.3	11.4	12.5	8.7
289,971	155,572	189,167	175,084	168,324	55,041	161,039	217,223	265,567	207,922
2.0	1.8	1.8	1.6	1.6	1.4	1.4	1.4	1.3	...
32.6	37.7	44.0	49.7	55.2	56.8	62.1	69.9	78.7	85.7
7	7	7	7	7	6	6	6	6	6
391,105	462,008	557,807	679,161	818,538	944,049	1,084,308	1,293,405	1,551,022	1,794,430
35.0	18.1	20.7	21.7	20.5	15.3	14.8	19.3	19.9	15.7
604,332	688,934	782,321	835,843	864,719	793,681	814,164	822,077	829,291	789,041
45.3	14.0	13.6	6.8	3.5	-8.2	2.6	1.0	0.9	-4.9
...	...	...	...	...	...	...	...	...	...
74,539	116,183	171,256	224,832	293,987	371,080	466,111	653,039[b] 777,921[c]	817,675[b] 981,386[c]	1,232,195
22.2	55.9	47.4	31.3	30.8	26.2	25.6	40.1[b] ...[c]	25.2[b] 26.2[c]	25.6
921,038	1,034,966	1,169,060	1,290,568	1,389,737	1,367,685	1,433,693	1,463,988[b] 1,339,106[c]	1,564,919[b] 1,401,208[c]	1,358,321
42.9	12.4	13.0	10.4	7.7	-1.6	4.8	2.1[b] ...[c]	6.9[b] 4.6[c]	-3.1
7.5	10.1	12.8	14.8	17.5	21.3	24.5	30.8[b] 36.7[c]	34.3[b] 41.2[c]	47.6
92.5	89.9	87.2	85.2	82.5	78.7	75.5	69.2[b] 63.3[c]	65.7[b] 58.8[c]	52.4
93,864	115,008	155,355	176,434	192,693	157,931	137,558	139,364	78,172[d]	52,000
13,457,613	13,184,652	13,985,014	13,512,028	12,426,675	10,393,113	11,238,697	11,878,793	9,194,492[d]	8,300,000
4,132,050	5,255,237	5,775,741	6,097,999	6,184,159	...	...	...	...	...
3,230,554	3,900,873	4,722,151	5,152,845	5,396,980	4,136,809	4,321,962	3,959,822	2,694,196[d]	2,331,000
41.1	15.6	16.4	13.1	11.1	-14.7	...	...	...	...
80.9	22.5	35.1	13.6	9.2	-18.0	-12.9	1.3	-43.9[d]	...
11.2	-2.0	6.1	-3.4	-8.0	-16.4	8.1	5.7	-23.0[d]	...
37.3	27.2	9.9	5.6	1.4	...	...	...	...	...

General Population, Agriculture, and Manufacturing Statistics, 1790-1970—SOUTH CAROLINA (Cont.)

Item No.	1790 (or 1789)	1800	1810	1820	1830	1840	1850	1860	1870*
26. Average acreage per farm[16]	...	...	...	...	...	...	541.2	488.2	233.3
27. Percentage increase in cropland harvested[16]	...	...	...	...	...	...	...	...	...
28. Value of farms, dollars[16]	...	...	...	...	...	...	82,431,684	139,652,508	35,847,010
29. Value of farms, percent increase[16]	...	...	...	...	...	...	...	69.4	-74.3
30. Average value per farm, dollars[16]	...	...	...	...	...	...	2,751	4,210	691
31. Farms operated by owners[19, 20, 21, 22, 23, 24]	...	...	...	...	...	...	...	...	...
32. Value of livestock on farms, dollars[25, 26, 27, 54]	...	...	...	...	...	...	15,060,015	23,934,465	9,954,808[g]
33. Average value of livestock per farm, dollars[25, 26, 27, 52, 54]	...	...	...	...	...	...	503	722	192[g]
34. Production of cotton in commercial bales[28, 29, 30, 31, 53]	...	...	...	...	...	...	300,901	353,412	224,500
35. Percent of total production of cotton[28, 29, 30, 31, 53]	...	...	...	...	...	...	12.2	6.6	7.5
36. Production of corn in bushels[32, 33, 34, 35, 53]	...	...	...	...	...	...	16,271,454	15,065,606	7,614,207
37. Percent of total production of corn[32, 33, 34, 35, 53]	...	...	...	...	...	...	2.8	1.8	1.0
38. Production of tobacco in pounds[36, 37, 38, 53]	...	...	...	...	...	...	74,285	104,412	34,805
39. Percent of total production of tobacco[36, 37, 38, 53]	...	...	...	...	...	...	0.1	...	...
40. Production of rice in pounds[39]	...	...	...	...	...	...	159,930,613	119,100,528	32,304,825
41. Production of rice in bushels[40, 41]	...	...	...	...	...	...	...	...	...
42. Percent of total production of rice[30, 40, 41]	...	...	...	...	...	...	74.3	63.6	43.9
43. Number of manufacturing establishments[42, 43, 44, 45, 46, 55]	...	...	...	...	...	...	1,430	1,230	1,584
44. Capital of manufacturing establishments[42, 43, 44]	...	...	...	...	...	...	6,053.265	6,931,756	5,400,418
45. Average number of wage earners[42, 43, 44, 45, 46, 55]	...	...	...	...	...	...	7,066	6,994	8,141
46. Total wages[42, 43, 45, 46, 55]	...	...	...	...	...	...	1,127,712	1,380,027	1,543,715
47. Cost of materials used in manufacturing[42, 43, 44, 45, 46, 55]	...	...	...	...	...	...	2,787,534	5,198,881	5,855,736
48. Value of manufactured product[42, 43, 44, 45, 46]	...	...	...	...	...	...	7,045,477	8,615,195	9,858,981

a. Membership of House of Representatives in 1789: 5.
b. Previous urban/rural definition. Rural included population residing outside of incorporated places having 2,500 inhabitants or more.
c. Current urban/rural definition. Urban includes those residing in urban-fringe areas and in unincorporated places of 2,500 or more.
d. For 1959
e. Based on a sampling of farms
f. Includes part owners
g. Values in gold
h. Computed on data available
i. For 1967

*The 1870 Census of population is considered incomplete in the Southern states.

General Population, Agriculture, and Manufacturing Statistics, 1790-1970—SOUTH CAROLINA (Cont.)

1880	1890	1900	1910	1920	1930	1940	1950	1960	1970
143.4	114.6	90.0	76.6	64.5	65.8	81.7	85.2	117.0[d]	...
...	20.7	21.1	9.1	4.7	-23.3	4.5	-8.4	-6.7[d]	...
68,677,482	99,104,600	126,761,530	332,888,081	813,484,200	379,190,630	338,494,517	820,349,000[e]	1,226,146,000[d,e]	...
91.6	44.3	27.9	162.6	144.4	-53.4	-10.7	142.3[e]	49.5[d,e]	...
732	862	816	1,887	4,222	2,401	2,461	5,886[e]	15,685[d,e]	...
46,645	51,428	60,471	64,350[f]	67,724[f]	54,470[f]	59,867[f]	75,777[f]	53,717[d,f]	...
12,199,510	16,572,410	20,199,859	45,131,380	91,133,474	38,888,439	43,092,480	72,268,009	77,363,569[d]	107,971,000
130	144	130	256	475	246	313	519	990[d]	2,076
522,548	747,190	881,422	1,279,866	1,476,645	835,963	849,982	543,936	411,120	211,000
9.1	10.0	9.2	12.0	13.0	5.7	7.4	3.5[h]	2.9[h]	2.1
11,767,099	13,770,417	17,429,610	20,871,946	27,472,013	19,325,825	23,527,406	23,624,155	24,975,000	10,854,000
0.7	0.6	0.7	0.8	1.2	0.9	1.0	0.8	0.6	0.3
45,678	222,898	19,895,970	25,583,049	71,193,072	83,302,706	118,962,944	61,263,001	81,254,720	141,075,000
...	0.1	2.3	2.4	5.2	5.7	7.0	7.1	7.8	7.4
52,077,515	30,338,951	47,360,128	...	...	...	...	...	...	...
...	...	...	541,570	122,465	29,203	16,078	...	...	...
47.3	23.6	16.7	2.4	0.3	0.1	...	...	...	...
2,078	2,382	3,762	1,854	2,004	1,659	1,331)			3,465[i]
11,205,894	29,276,261	67,356,465	173,221,000	374,538,000	...	...)			...
15,828	22,748	48,135	73,046	79,450	108,777	126,983)			304,300[i]
2,836,289	5,474,739	9,455,900	20,361,000	62,566,000	73,223,000	86,616,000)	See following table		1,502,200,000[i]
9,885,538	18,873,666	34,027,795	66,351,000	227,986,000	226,542,000	227,666,000)			3,448,500,000[i]
16,738,008	31,926,681	58,748,731	113,236,000	381,453,000	385,892,000	397,513,000)			...

General Population, Agriculture, and Manufacturing Statistics, 1790-1970

TENNESSEE

Item No.	1790 (or 1789)	1800	1810	1820	1830	1840	1850	1860	1870*
1. Population[1, 50]	35,691	105,602	261,727	422,823	681,904	829,210	1,002,717	1,109,801	1,258,520
2. Decennial rates of increase in population over preceding census[2, 50]	...	195.9	147.8	61.6	61.3	21.6	20.9	10.7	13.4
3. Increase in population over previous census[1, 3, 50]	...	69,911	156,125	161,096	259,081	147,306	173,507	107,084	148,719
4. Percent distribution of population[4]	0.9	2.0	3.6	4.4	5.3	4.9	4.3	3.5	3.3
5. Population per square mile of land area[5, 6, 50]	...	2.5	...	...	...	...	24.1	26.6	30.2
6. Membership of House of Representatives at each apportionment[7]	1	3	6	9	13	11	10	8	10
7. White population[8, 9, 10, 51]	31,913	91,709	215,875	339,979	535,746	640,627	756,836	826,722	936,119
8. Percentage increase in white population over preceding census[9, 10, 11, 51]	...	187.4	135.4	57.5	57.6	19.6	18.1	9.2	13.2
9. Negro population[8, 9, 10, 51]	3,778	13,893	45,852	82,844	146,158	188,583	245,881	283,019	322,331
10. Percentage increase in Negro population over preceding census[9, 10, 11, 12, 13, 51]	...	267.7	230.0	80.7	76.4	29.0	30.4	15.1	13.9
11. Number of slaves in the area enumerated in 1790 and in the added area[14]	3,417	13,584	44,535	80,107	141,603	183,059	239,459	275,719	...
12. Urban population[15, 50]	...	...	...	...	5,566	6,929	21,983	46,541	94,237
13. Percent urban increase over preceding census[15, 50]	...	...	...	...	...	24.5	217.3	111.7	102.5
14. Rural population[15, 50]	35,691	105,602	261,727	422,823	676,338	822,281	980,734	1,063,260	1,164,283
15. Percent rural increase over preceding census[15, 50]	...	195.9	147.8	61.6	60.0	21.6	19.3	8.4	9.5
16. Percent of urban to total population[15, 50]	...	...	...	...	0.8	0.8	2.2	4.2	7.5
17. Percent of rural to total population[15, 50]	100.0	100.0	100.0	100.0	99.2	99.2	97.8	95.8	92.5
18. Number of farms[16, 52]	...	...	...	...	...	...	72,735	82,368	118,141
19. Acres in farms[16, 52]	...	...	...	...	...	...	18,984,022	20,669,165	19,581,214
20. Acres improved land in farms[17]	...	...	...	...	...	...	5,175,173	6,795,337	6,843,278
21. Cropland harvested, acres[16, 53]	...	...	...	...	...	...	...	...	...
22. Percentage increase in farm population[17, 18]	...	...	...	...	...	...	...	10.7	13.4
23. Percentage increase in number of farms[16, 17]	...	...	...	...	...	...	...	13.2	43.4
24. Percentage increase of land in farms[16, 17]	...	...	...	...	...	...	...	8.9	-5.3
25. Percentage increase of improved land in farms[17]	...	...	...	...	...	...	...	31.3	0.7

General Population, Agriculture, and Manufacturing Statistics, 1790-1970

TENNESSEE

1880	1890	1900	1910	1920	1930	1940	1950	1960	1970
1,542,359	1,767,518	2,020,616	2,184,789	2,337,885	2,616,556	2,915,841	3,291,718	3,567,089	3,923,687
22.6	14.6	14.3	8.1	7.0	11.9	11.4	12.9	8.4	10.0
283,839	225,159	253,098	164,173	153,096	278,671	299,285	375,877	275,371	356,598
3.1	2.8	2.7	2.4	2.2	2.1	2.2	2.2	2.0	...
37.0	42.4	48.5	52.4	56.1	62.4	69.5	78.8	85.4	94.9
10	10	10	10	10	9	10	9	9	8
1,138,831	1,336,637	1,540,186	1,711,432	1,885,993	2,138,644	2,406,906	2,760,257	2,977,753	3,293,930
21.7	17.4	15.2	11.1	10.2	13.4	12.5	14.7	7.9	10.6
403,151	430,678	480,243	473,088	451,758	477,646	508,736	530,603	586,876	621,261
25.1	6.8	11.5	-1.5	-4.5	5.7	6.5	4.3	10.6	5.9
...	...	...	...	...	...	...	...	...	...
115,984	238,394	326,639	441,045	611,226	896,538	1,027,206	1,264,159[a] 1,452,602[b]	1,631,698[a] 1,864,828[b]	2,305,307
23.1	105.5	37.0	35.0	38.6	46.7	14.6	23.1[a] ...[b]	29.1[a] 28.4[b]	23.6
1,426,375	1,529,124	1,693,977	1,743,744	1,726,659	1,720,018	1,888,635	2,027,559[a] 1,839,116[b]	1,935,391[a] 1,702,261[b]	1,618,380
22.5	7.2	10.8	2.9	-1.0	-0.4	9.8	7.4[a] ...[b]	-4.5[a] -7.4[b]	-4.9
7.5	13.5	16.2	20.2	26.1	34.3	35.2	38.4[a] 44.1[b]	45.7[a] 52.3[b]	58.8
92.5	86.5	83.8	79.8	73.9	65.7	64.8	61.6[a] 55.9[b]	54.3[a] 47.7[b]	41.2
165,650	174,412	224,623	246,012	252,774	245,657	247,617	231,631	157,688[c]	127,000
20,666,915	20,161,583	20,342,058	20,041,657	19,510,856	18,003,241	18,492,898	18,534,380	16,081,285[c]	15,500,000
8,496,556	9,362,555	10,245,950	10,890,484	11,185,302	...	...	...	...	...
5,601,179	5,777,345	6,680,504	6,365,143	6,787,384	6,106,300	6,158,662	5,575,106	4,116,418[c]	4,031,000
22.6	14.6	14.3	8.1	7.0	-4.4	...	...	...	...
40.2	5.3	28.8	9.5	2.7	-2.8	0.8	-6.4	-31.9[c]	...
5.5	-2.4	0.9	-1.5	-2.6	-7.7	2.7	0.2	-13.2[c]	...
24.2	10.2	9.4	6.3	2.7	...	...	...	...	...

General Population, Agriculture, and Manufacturing Statistics, 1790-1970—TENNESSEE (Cont.)

Item No.	1790 (or 1789)	1800	1810	1820	1830	1840	1850	1860	1870*
26. Average acreage per farm[16]	...	...	...	...	...	...	261.0	250.9	165.7
27. Percentage increase in cropland harvested[16]	...	...	...	...	...	...	...	...	...
28. Value of farms, dollars[16]	...	...	...	...	...	...	97,851,212	271,358,985	174,994,997
29. Value of farms, percent increase[16]	...	...	...	...	...	...	...	177.3	-35.5
30. Average value per farm, dollars[16]	...	...	...	...	...	...	1,345	3,294	1,481
31. Farms operated by owners[19, 20, 21, 22, 23, 24]	...	...	...	...	...	...	...	...	...
32. Value of livestock on farms, dollars[25, 26, 27, 54]	...	...	...	...	...	...	29,978,016	60,211,425	44,067,260[f]
33. Average value of livestock per farm, dollars[25, 26, 27, 52, 54]	...	...	...	...	...	...	412	731	373[f]
34. Production of cotton in commercial bales[28, 29, 30, 31, 53]	...	...	...	...	...	...	194,532	296,464	181,842
35. Percent of total production of cotton[28, 29, 30, 31, 53]	...	...	...	...	...	...	7.9	5.5	6.0
36. Production of corn in bushels[32, 33, 34, 35, 53]	...	...	...	...	...	...	52,276,223	52,089,926	41,343,614
37. Percent of total production of corn[32, 33, 34, 35, 53]	...	...	...	...	...	...	8.8	6.2	5.4
38. Production of tobacco in pounds[36, 37, 38, 53]	...	...	...	...	...	...	20,148,932	43,448,097	21,465,452
39. Percent of total production of tobacco[36, 37, 38, 53]	...	...	...	...	...	...	10.1	10.0	8.2
40. Production of rice in pounds[39]	...	...	...	...	...	...	258,854	40,372	3,399
41. Production of rice in bushels[40, 41]	...	...	...	...	...	...	...	...	...
42. Percent of total production of rice[39, 40, 41]	...	...	...	...	...	...	0.1	...	...
43. Number of manufacturing establishments[42, 43, 44, 45, 46, 55]	...	...	...	...	...	...	2,887	2,572	5,317
44. Capital of manufacturing establishments[42, 43, 44]	...	...	...	...	...	...	6,527,729	14,426,261	15,595,295
45. Average number of wage earners[42, 43, 44, 45, 46, 55]	...	...	...	...	...	...	12,039	12,528	19,412
46. Total wages[42, 43, 45, 46, 55]	...	...	...	...	...	...	2,247,492	3,370,687	5,390,630
47. Cost of materials used in manufacturing[42, 43, 44, 45, 46, 55]	...	...	...	...	...	...	5,166,886	9,416,514	19,657,027
48. Value of manufactured product[42, 43, 44, 45, 46]	...	...	...	...	...	...	9,725,608	17,987,225	34,362,636

a. Previous urban/rural definition. Rural included population residing outside of incorporated places having 2,500 inhabitants or more.
b. Current urban/rural definition. Urban includes those residing in urban-fringe areas and in unincorporated places of 2,500 or more.
c. For 1959
d. Based on a sampling of farms
e. Includes part owners
f. Values in gold
g. Gased on data available
h. For 1967

*The 1870 Census of population is considered incomplete in the Southern states.

1880	1890	1900	1910	1920	1930	1940	1950	1960	1970
124.8	115.6	90.6	81.5	77.2	73.3	74.7	80.0	102.0[c]	...
...	3.1	15.6	-4.7	6.6	-10.0	0.8	-9.5	-26.2[c]	...
206,749,837	242,700,540	265,150,750	480,522,587	1,024,979,894	743,222,363	664,474,267	1,431,966,000[d]	2,095,354,000[c, d]	...
18.1	17.4	9.3	81.2	113.3	-27.5	-10.6	115.5[d]	46.3[c, d]	...
1,248	1,392	1,180	1,953	4,055	3,025	2,683	6,182[d]	13,288[c, d]	...
108,454	120,622	133,483	144,125[e]	148,082[e]	131,526[e]	147,443[e]	163,521[e]	127,134[c, e]	...
43,651,470	60,254,230	60,818,605	110,706,078	171,931,245	104,252,201	97,706,469	215,817,363	256,564,677[c]	403,401,000
264	345	271	450	686	424	395	932	1,627[c]	3,176
330,621	190,579	234,592	264,562	306,974	503,816	436,126	616,742	620,385	392,000
5.7	2.5	2.5	2.5	2.7	3.4	3.8	4.0[g]	4.4[g]	3.9
62,764,429	63,635,350	67,307,390	67,682,489	70,639,252	61,045,986	54,904,608	56,099,664	65,560,000	22,760,000
3.6	3.0	2.5	2.6	3.0	2.9	2.4	2.0	1.5	0.6
29,365,052	36,368,395	49,157,550	68,756,599	112,367,567	112,236,961	109,422,777	127,324,176	120,652,665	114,269,000
6.2	7.5	5.7	6.5	8.2	7.7	6.4	7.2	7.3	6.0
...	...	...	...	...	...	...	...	...	...
...	...	...	...	...	...	...	...	...	...
...	...	...	...	...	...	...	...	...	...
4,326	4,559	8,016	4,609	4,589	2,855	2,289)			5,040[h]
20,092,845	51,475,092	71,814,038	167,924,000	410,203,000	...	...)			...
22,445	37,487	50,504	73,840	95,167	128,400	131,874)			418,000[h]
5,254,775	13,557,180	16,647,638	28,251,000	81,355,000	115,877,000	109,662,000)	See following table		2,190,000,000[h]
23,834,262	40,463,782	63,857,511	104,016,000	344,767,000	407,611,000	407,746,000)			5,848,000,000[h]
37,074,886	72,355,286	108,144,565	180,217,000	556,253,000	730,509,000	728,088,000)			...

General Population, Agriculture, and Manufacturing Statistics, 1790-1970

TEXAS

Item No.	1790 (or 1789)	1800	1810	1820	1830	1840	1850	1860	1870*
1. Population[1, 50]	...	...	...	...	...	...	212,592	604,215	818,579
2. Decennial rates of increase in population over preceding census[2, 50]	...	...	...	...	...	...	...	184.2	35.5
3. Increase in population over previous census[1, 3, 50]	...	...	...	...	...	...	212,592	391,623	214,364
4. Percent distribution of population[4]	...	...	...	...	...	...	0.9	1.9	2.1
5. Population per square mile of land area[5, 6, 50]	...	...	...	...	...	...	0.8	2.3	3.1
6. Membership of House of Representatives at each apportionment[7]	...	...	...	...	...	2	2	4	6
7. White population[8, 9, 10, 51]	...	...	...	...	...	...	154,034	420,891	564,700
8. Percentage increase in white population over preceding census[9, 10, 11, 51]	...	...	...	...	...	...	...	173.2	34.2
9. Negro population[8, 9, 10, 51]	...	...	...	...	...	...	58,558	182,921	253,475
10. Percentage increase in Negro population over preceding census[9, 10, 11, 12, 13, 51]	...	...	...	...	...	...	...	212.4	38.6
11. Number of slaves in the area enumerated in 1790 and in the added area[14]	...	...	...	...	...	...	58,161	182,566	...
12. Urban population[15, 50]	...	...	...	...	...	...	7,665	26,615	54,521
13. Percent urban increase over preceding census[15, 50]	...	...	...	...	...	...	...	247.2	104.9
14. Rural population[15, 50]	...	...	...	...	...	...	204,927	577,600	764,058
15. Percent rural increase over preceding census[15, 50]	...	...	...	...	...	...	...	181.9	32.3
16. Percent of urban to total population[15, 50]	...	...	...	...	...	...	3.6	4.4	6.7
17. Percent of rural to total population[15, 50]	...	...	...	...	...	...	96.4	95.6	93.3
18. Number of farms[16, 52]	...	...	...	...	...	...	12,198	42,891	61,125
19. Acres in farms[16, 52]	...	...	...	...	...	...	11,496,339	25,344,028	18,396,523
20. Acres improved land in farms[17]	...	...	...	...	...	...	643,976	2,650,781	2,964,836
21. Cropland harvested, acres[16, 53]	...	...	...	...	...	...	...	...	...
22. Percentage increase in farm population[17, 18]	...	...	...	...	...	...	...	184.2	35.5
23. Percentage increase in number of farms[16, 17]	...	...	...	...	...	...	...	251.6	42.5
24. Percentage increase of land in farms[16, 17]	...	...	...	...	...	...	...	120.5	-27.4
25. Percentage increase of improved land in farms[17]	...	...	...	...	...	...	...	311.6	11.8

TEXAS

1880	1890	1900	1910	1920	1930	1940	1950	1960	1970
1,591,749	2,235,527	3,048,710	3,896,542	4,663,228	5,824,715	6,414,824	7,711,194	9,579,677	11,196,730
94.5	40.4	36.4	27.8	19.7	24.9	10.1	20.2	24.2	16.9
773,170	643,774	813,187	847,832	766,686	1,161,487	590,109	1,296,370	1,868,483	1,617,053
3.2	3.5	4.0	4.2	4.4	4.7	4.9	5.1	5.3	...
6.1	8.5	11.6	14.8	17.8	22.1	24.3	29.3	36.5	42.7
11	13	16	18	18	21	21	22	23	24
1,197,237	1,745,935	2,426,669	3,204,848	3,918,165	4,967,172	5,487,545	6,726,534	8,374,831	9,717,128
112.0	45.8	39.0	32.1	22.3	26.8	10.5	22.6	24.5	16.0
393,384	488,171	620,722	690,049	741,694	854,964	924,391	977,458	1,187,125	1,399,005
55.2	24.1	27.2	11.2	7.5	15.3	8.1	5.7	21.4	17.8
...	...	...	...	...	...	...	...	...	...
146,795	349,511	520,759	938,104	1,512,689	2,389,348	2,917,389	4,612,666[a] 4,838,060[b]	9,963,114[a] 7,187,470[b]	8,920,946
169.2	138.1	49.0	80.1	61.2	58.0	21.8	58.4[a] ...[b]	51.0[a] 48.6[b]	24.1
1,444,954	1,886,016	2,527,951	2,958,438	3,150,539	3,435,367	3,503,435	3,098,528[a] 2,873,134[b]	2,616,563[a] 2,392,207[b]	2,275,784
89.1	30.5	34.0	17.0	6.5	9.0	2.0	-11.6[a] ...[b]	-15.6[a] -16.7[b]	-4.9
9.2	15.6	17.1	24.1	32.4	41.0	45.4	59.8[a] 62.7[b]	72.7[a] 75.0[b]	79.7
90.8	84.4	82.9	75.9	67.6	59.0	54.6	40.2[a] 37.3[b]	27.3[a] 25.0[b]	20.3
174,184	228,126	352,190	417,770	436,033	495,489	418,002	331,567	227,071[c]	188,000
36,292,219	51,406,937	125,807,017	112,435,067	114,020,621	124,707,130	137,683,372	145,389,014	143,217,559[c]	145,000,000
12,650,314	20,746,215	19,576,076	27,360,666	31,227,503	...	...	...	...	...
5,356,360	8,393,489	15,112,549	18,389,092	25,030,834	30,634,370	26,044,008	28,107,865	22,236,473[c]	19,131,000
94.5	40.4	36.4	27.8	19.7	3.3	...	...	...	...
185.0	31.0	54.4	18.6	4.4	13.6	-15.6	-20.7	-31.5[c]	...
97.3	41.6	144.7	-10.6	1.4	9.4	10.4	5.6	-1.5[c]	...
326.7	64.0	-5.6	39.8	14.1	...	...	...	...	...

Item No.	1790 (or 1789)	1800	1810	1820	1830	1840	1850	1860	1870*
26. Average acreage per farm [16]	...	...	...	...	...	...	942.5	590.9	301.0
27. Percentage increase in cropland harvested [16]	...	...	...	...	...	...	...	...	...
28. Value of farms, dollars [16]	...	...	...	...	...	...	16,550,008	88,101,320	48,119,960
29. Value of farms, percent increase [16]	...	...	...	...	...	...	...	432.3	-45.4
30. Average value per farm, dollars [16]	...	...	...	...	...	...	1,357	2,054	787
31. Farms operated by owners [19, 20, 21, 22, 23, 24]	...	...	...	...	...	...	...	...	...
32. Value of livestock on farms, dollars [25, 26, 27, 54]	...	...	...	...	...	...	10,412,927	42,825,447	29,940,155[f]
33. Average value of livestock per farm, dollars [25, 26, 27, 52, 54]	...	...	...	...	...	...	854	998	490[f]
34. Production of cotton in commercial bales [28, 29, 30, 31, 53]	...	...	...	...	...	...	58,072	431,463	350,628
35. Percent of total production of cotton [28, 29, 30, 31, 53]	...	...	...	...	...	...	2.4	8.0	11.6
36. Production of corn in bushels [32, 33, 34, 35, 53]	...	...	...	...	...	...	6,028,876	16,500,702	20,554,538
37. Percent of total production of corn [32, 33, 34, 35, 53]	...	...	...	...	...	...	1.0	2.0	2.7
38. Production of tobacco in pounds [36, 37, 38]	...	...	...	...	...	...	66,897	97,914	59,706
39. Percent of total production of tobacco [36, 37, 58]	...	...	...	...	...	...	...	...	...
40. Production of rice in pounds [39, 53]	...	...	...	...	...	...	88,203	26,031	63,844
41. Production of rice in bushels [40, 41]	...	...	...	...	...	...	...	...	...
42. Percent of total production of rice [39, 40, 41, 53]	...	...	...	...	...	...	...	...	0.1
43. Number of manufacturing establishments [42, 43, 44, 45, 46, 55]	...	...	...	...	...	...	309	983	2,399
44. Capital of manufacturing establishments [42, 43, 44]	...	...	...	...	...	...	539,290	3,272,450	5,284,110
45. Average number of wage earners [42, 43, 44, 45, 46, 55]	...	...	...	...	...	...	1,066	3,449	7,927
46. Total wages [42, 43, 45, 46, 55]	...	...	...	...	...	...	322,368	1,162,756	1,787,835
47. Cost of materials used in manufacturing [42, 43, 44, 45, 46, 55]	...	...	...	...	...	...	394,642	3,367,372	6,273,193
48. Value of manufactured product [42, 43, 44, 45, 46]	...	...	...	...	...	...	1,168,538	6,577,202	11,517,302

a. Previous urban/rural definition. Rural included population residing outside of incorporated places having 2,500 inhabitants or more.
b. Current urban/rural definition. Urban includes those residing in urban-fringe areas and in unincorporated places of 2,500 or more.
c. For 1959.
d. Based on a sampling of farms
e. Includes part owners
f. Values in gold
g. Including estimated value of range animals
h. Based on data available
i. For 1967

*The 1870 Census of population is considered incomplete in the Southern States.

General Population, Agriculture, and Manufacturing Statistics, 1790-1970—TEXAS (Cont.)

1880	1890	1900	1910	1920	1930	1940	1950	1960	1970
208.4	225.3	357.2	269.1	261.5	251.7	329.4	438.5	630.7[c]	...
...	56.7	80.1	21.7	36.1	22.4	-15.0	7.9	-20.9[c]	...
170,468,886	399,971,289	691,773,613	1,843,208,395	3,700,173,319	3,597,406,986	2,589,978,936	6,718,426,000[d]	11,759,366,000[c,d]	...
254.2	134.6	73.0	166.4	100.7	-2.8	-28.0	159.4[d]	75.0[c,d]	...
979	1,753	1,964	4,412	8,486	7,260	6,196	20,263[d]	51,787[c,d]	...
108,716	132,616	177,199	195,863[e]	201,210[e]	190,515[e]	210,182[e]	228,372[e]	178,049[c,e]	...
76,563,987[g]	138,409,274[g]	240,576,955	318,646,509	590,531,879	453,716,794	344,946,306	1,019,560,574	1,244,715,031[c]	1,996,142,000
440	607	683	763	1,360	916	825	3,075	5,482[c]	10,617
805,284	1,471,242	2,506,212	2,455,174	2,971,757	3,793,392	2,724,442	5,549,667	4,155,986	3,213,900
14.0	19.7	26.3	23.0	26.1	26.0	23.7	36.0[h]	29.9[h]	31.6
29,065,172	69,112,150	109,970,350	75,498,695	108,377,282	66,251,026	69,649,829	44,077,397	42,728,000	33,232,000
1.7	3.3	4.1	2.9	4.6	3.1	3.0	1.6	1.0	0.8
221,283	175,706	550,120	161,533	27,067	7,584	2,715	...	...	...
0.1	...	...	...	...	...	...	...	...	...
62,152	108,423	7,186,863	...	...	...	...	...	...	2,101,500,000
...	...	...	8,991,745	5,306,369	5,158,544	10,396,901	23,919,372	30,240,504	...
0.1	0.1	2.5	39.5	14.7	15.3	23.7	26.7[h]	25.0[h]	25.1
2,996	5,268	12,289	4,588	5,724	5,198	5,376)			12,722[i]
9,245,561	46,815,181	90,433,882	216,876,000	585,776,000	...	...)			...
12,159	34,794	48,153	70,230	107,522	134,498	126,992)			657,500[i]
3,343,087	15,148,495	20,552,355	37,907,000	116,404,000	151,827,000	128,139,000)			4,340,400,000[i]
12,956,269	36,152,308	67,102,769	178,178,000	701,171,000	989,940,000	1,077,115,000)			15,785,000,000[i]
20,719,928	70,433,551	119,414,982	272,896,000	999,996,000	1,450,246,000	1,530,221,000)			...

General Population, Agriculture, and Manufacturing Statistics, 1790-1970

VIRGINA

Item No.	1790 (or 1789)	1800	1810	1820	1830	1840	1850	1860	1870*
1. Population[1, 50]	691,737[a]	807,557[a]	877,683[a]	938,261[a]	1,044,054[a]	1,025,227[a]	1,119,348[a]	1,219,630[a]	1,225,163
2. Decennial rates of increase in population over preceding census[2, 50]	...	16.7	8.7	6.9	11.3	-1.8	9.2	9.0	0.5
3. Increase in population over previous census[1, 3, 50]	...	115,820[a]	70,126[a]	60,578[a]	105,793[a]	-18,827[a]	94,121[a]	100,282[a]	5,533
4. Percent distribution of population[4]	17.6	15.2	12.1	9.7	8.1	6.0	4.8	3.9	3.2
5. Population per square mile of land area[5, 6, 50]	...	13.7	...	...	...	...	22.1	24.8	30.4
6. Membership of House of Representatives at each apportionment[7]	19[b]	22	23	22	21	15	13	11	9
7. White population[8, 9, 10, 51]	442,117[c]	514,280[c]	551,514[c]	603,335[c]	694,300[c]	740,968[c]	894,800[c]	1,047,299[c]	712,089
8. Percentage increase in white population over preceding census[9, 10, 11, 51]	...	16.3	7.2	9.4	15.1	6.7	20.8	17.0	-32.0
9. Negro population[8, 9, 10, 51]	305,493[c]	365,920[c]	423,086[c]	462,031[c]	517,105[c]	498,829[c]	526,861[c]	548,907[c]	512,841
10. Percentage increase in Negro population over preceding census[9, 10, 11, 12, 13, 51]	...	19.8	15.6	9.2	11.9	-3.5	5.6	4.2	-6.6
11. Number of slaves in the area enumerated in 1790 and in the added area[14]	287,959[a]	339,796[a, d]	383,521[a, d]	411,886[a, d]	453,698[a, d]	431,873[a, d]	452,028[a]	472,494[a]	...
12. Urban population[15, a, 50]	12,296	21,155	31,823	35,453	50,375	70,968	89,255	115,879	145,618
13. Percent urban increase over preceding census[15, 50]	...	72.0	50.4	11.4	42.1	40.9	25.8	29.8	25.7
14. Rural population[15, a, 50]	679,441	786,402	845,860	902,808	993,679	954,259	1,030,093	1,103,751	1,079,545
15. Percent rural increase over preceding census[15, 50]	...	15.7	7.6	6.7	10.1	-4.0	7.9	7.2	-2.2
16. Percent of urban to total population[15, 50]	1.8	2.6	3.6	3.8	4.8	6.9	8.0	9.5	11.9
17. Percent of rural to total population[15, 50]	98.2	97.4	96.4	96.2	95.2	93.1	92.0	90.5	88.1
18. Number of farms[16, 52]	...	...	...	...	...	...	77,013[c]	92,605[c]	73,849
19. Acres in farms[16, 52]	...	...	...	...	...	...	26,152,311[c]	31,117,036[c]	18,145,911
20. Acres improved land in farms[17]	...	...	...	...	...	...	10,360,135[c]	11,437,821[c]	8,165,040
21. Cropland harvested, acres[16, 53]	...	...	...	...	...	...	...	...	...
22. Percentage increase in farm population[17, 18]	...	...	...	...	...	...	...	12.3[c]	-23.3
23. Percentage increase in number of farms[16, 17]	...	...	...	...	...	...	...	20.2[c]	-20.3
24. Percentage increase of land in farms[16, 17]	...	...	...	...	...	...	...	19.0[c]	-41.7
25. Percentage increase of improved land in farms[17]	...	...	...	...	...	...	...	10.4[c]	-28.6

General Population, Agriculture, and Manufacturing Statistics, 1790-1970

VIRGINIA

	1880	1890	1900	1910	1920	1930	1940	1950	1960	1970
	1,512,565	1,655,980	1,854,184	2,061,612	2,309,187	2,421,851	2,677,773	3,318,680	3,966,949	4,648,494
	23.5	9.5	12.0	11.2	12.0	4.9	10.6	23.9	19.5	17.2
	287,402	143,415	198,204	207,428	247,575	112,664	255,922	640,907	648,269	681,545
	3.0	2.6	2.4	2.2	2.2	2.0	2.0	2.2	2.2	. . .
	37.6	41.1	46.1	51.2	57.4	60.7	67.1	83.2	99.6	116.9
	10	10	10	10	10	9	9	10	10	10
	880,858	1,020,122	1,192,855	1,389,809	1,617,909	1,770,441	2,015,583	2,581,555	3,142,443	3,761,514
	23.7	15.8	16.9	16.5	16.4	9.4	13.8	28.1	21.7	19.7
	631,616	635,438	660,722	671,096	690,017	650,165	661,449	734,211	816,258	861,368
	23.2	0.6	4.0	1.6	2.8	-5.8	1.7	11.0	11.2	5.5
	. . .	. . .	. . .	. . .	. . .	. . .	. . .	. . .	. . .	. . .
	189,079	282,721	340,067	476,529	673,984	785,537	944,675	1,375,036[e] 1,560,115[f]	1,932,468[e] 2,204,913[f]	2,934,841
	29.8	49.5	20.3	40.1	41.4	16.6	20.3	45.6[e] . . .[f]	40.5[e] 41.3[f]	33.1
	1,323,486	1,373,259	1,514,117	1,585,083	1,635,203	1,636,314	1,733,098	1,943,644[e] 1,758,565[f]	2,034,481[e] 1,762,036[f]	1,713,653
	22.6	3.8	10.3	4.7	3.2	0.1	5.9	12.1[e] . . .[f]	4.7[e] 0.2[f]	-2.8
	12.5	17.1	18.3	23.1	29.2	32.4	35.3	41.4[e] 47.0[f]	48.7[e] 55.6[f]	63.1
	87.5	82.9	81.7	76.9	70.8	67.6	64.7	58.6[e] 53.0[f]	51.3[e] 44.4[f]	36.9
	118,517	127,600	167,886	184,018	186,242	170,610	174,885	150,997	97,623[g]	72,000
	19,835,785	19,104,951	19,907,883	19,495,636	18,561,112	16,728,620	16,444,907	15,572,295	13,125,802[g]	11,500,000
	8,510,113	9,125,545	10,094,805	9,870,058	9,460,492	. . .	. . .	. . .	. . .	. . .
	3,844,702	3,781,053	4,345,537	4,256,226	4,579,830	3,975,307	3,840,189	3,313,849	2,857,848[g]	2,666,000
	23.5	9.5	12.0	11.2	12.0	-10.7	. . .	. . .	. . .	. . .
	60.5	7.7	31.6	9.6	1.2	-8.4	2.5	-13.6	-35.3[g]	. . .
	9.3	-3.7	4.2	-2.1	-4.8	-9.9	-1.7	-5.3	-15.7[g]	. . .
	4.2	7.2	10.6	-2.2	-4.1	. . .	. . .	. . .	. . .	. . .

General Population, Agriculture, and Manufacturing Statistics, 1790-1970—VIRGINIA (Cont.)

Item No.	1790 (or 1789)	1800	1810	1820	1830	1840	1850	1860	1870*
26. Average acreage per farm[16]	...	...	...	...	...	...	339.6[c]	336.0[c]	245.7
27. Percentage increase in cropland harvested[16]	...	...	...	...	...	...	...	...	...
28. Value of farms, dollars[16]	...	...	...	...	...	...	216,401,543[c]	371,761,661[c]	170,416,676
29. Value of farms, percent increase[16]	...	...	...	...	...	...	...	71.8[c]	-54.2
30. Average value per farm, dollars[16]	...	...	...	...	...	...	2,810[c]	4,014[c]	2,308
31. Farms operated by owners[19, 20, 21, 22, 23, 24]	...	...	...	...	...	...	...	...	...
32. Value of livestock on farms, dollars[25, 26, 27, 54]	...	...	...	...	...	...	33,656,659[c]	47,803,049[c]	22,550,135[j]
33. Average value of livestock per farm, dollars[25, 26, 27, 52, 54]	...	...	...	...	...	...	437[c]	516[c]	305[j]
34. Production of cotton in commercial bales[28, 29, 30, 31, 53]	...	...	...	...	...	...	3,947	12,727	183
35. Percent of total production of cotton[28, 29, 30, 31, 53]	...	...	...	...	...	...	0.2	0.2	...
36. Production of corn in bushels[32, 33, 34, 35, 53]	...	...	...	...	...	...	35,254,319[c]	38,319,999[c]	17,649,304
37. Percent of total production of corn[32, 33, 34, 35, 53]	...	...	...	...	...	...	6.0[c]	4.6[c]	2.3
38. Production of tobacco in pounds[36, 37, 38, 53]	...	...	...	...	...	...	56,803,227[c]	123,968,312[c]	37,086,364
39. Percent of total production of tobacco[36, 37, 38, 53]	...	...	...	...	...	...	28.4[c]	28.6[c]	14.1
40. Production of rice in pounds[39]	...	...	...	...	...	...	17,154[c]	8,225[c]	...
41. Production of rice in bushels[40, 41]	...	...	...	...	...	...	...	...	...
42. Percent of total production of rice[39, 40, 41]	...	...	...	...	...	...	...	...	...
43. Number of manufacturing establishments[42, 43, 44, 45, 46, 55]	...	...	...	...	...	...	4,740	5,385	5,933
44. Capital of manufacturing establishments[42, 43, 44]	...	...	...	...	...	...	18,109,143	26,935,560	18,455,400
45. Average number of wage earners[42, 43, 44, 45, 46, 55]	...	...	...	...	...	...	29,110	36,174	26,974
46. Total wages[42, 43, 45, 46, 55]	...	...	...	...	...	...	5,434,476	8,544,117	5,343,099
47. Cost of materials used in manufacturing[42, 43, 44, 45, 46, 55]	...	...	...	...	...	...	18,101,131	30,840,531	23,832,384
48. Value of manufactured product[42, 43, 44, 45, 46]	...	...	...	...	...	...	29,602,507	50,652,124	38,364,322

a. Excludes the area later set off as West Virginia
b. Membership of House of Representatives in 1789; 10
c. Includes the area later set off as West Virginia
d. Alexandria County, which from 1800 to 1840 inclusive formed a part of the District of Columbia, is included with Virginia.
e. Previous urban/rural definition. Rural included population residing outside of incorporated places having 2,500 inhabitants or more.
f. Current urban/rural definition. Urban includes those residing in urban-fringe areas and in unincorporated places of 2,500 or more.
g. For 1959
h. Based on a asampling of farms
i. Includes part owners
j. Values in gold
k. Based on data available
l. Less than .1%
m. For 1967
*The 1870 Census of population is considered incomplete in the Southern states.

General Population, Agriculture, and Manufacturing Statistics, 1790-1970—VIRGINIA (Cont.)

1880	1890	1900	1910	1920	1930	1940	1950	1960	1970
167.4	149.7	118.6	105.9	99.7	98.1	94.0	103.1	134.5[g]	...
...	-1.7	14.9	-2.1	7.6	-13.2	-3.4	-13.7	-13.8[g]	...
216,028,107	254,490,600	271,578,200	532,058,062	1,024,435,025	855,849,672	674,975,424	1,277,084,000[h]	1,819,248,000[g, h]	...
26.8	17.8	6.7	95.9	92.5	-16.4	-21.1	89.2[h]	42.4[g, h]	...
1,823	1,994	1,618	2,891	5,501	5,016	3,860	8,458[h]	18,635[g, h]	...
83,531	93,311	116,290	133,664[i]	136,363[i]	121,104[i]	126,674[i]	124,547[i]	82,959[g, i]	...
25,953,315	33,404,281	42,026,737	74,891,438	121,169,971	92,128,480	73,061,191	186,707,909	214,725,607[g]	269,201,000
219	262	250	407	655	540	418	1,237	2,200[g]	3,739
19,595	5,375	10,789	10,480	24,887	52,442	12,865	18,722	12,476	3,400
0.3	0.1	0.1	0.1	0.2	0.3	0.1	0.1[k]	0.1[k]	**[i]
29,119,761	27,172,493	36,748,410	38,295,141	42,302,978	32,772,810	33,600,920	33,150,002	37,352,000	31,144,000
1.7	1.3	1.4	1.5	1.8	1.5	1.4	1.2	0.9	0.8
79,988,868	48,522,655	122,884,900	132,979,390	102,391,226	115,825,610	136,753,568	124,904,164	127,795,512	125,844,000
16.9	9.9	14.2	12.6	7.5	7.9	8.0	7.0	7.8	6.6
...	360	4,374	...	...	...	...	...	...	...
...	...	...	...	...	...	...	...	...	...
...	...	...	...	...	...	...	...	...	...
5,710	5,915	8,248	5,685	5,603	3,287	2,579)			4,938[m]
26,968,990	63,456,799	103,670,988	216,392,000	463,645,000	...	...)			...
40,184	53,566	72,702	105,676	119,352	120,273	133,894)	See following table		339,800[m]
7,425,261	15,816,930	22,445,720	38,154,000	120,007,000	118,089,000	115,539,000)			1,905,100,000[m]
32,883,933	50,148,285	74,851,757	125,583,000	371,541,000	365,824,000	609,325,000)			4,543,000,000[m]
51,780,992	88,363,824	132,172,910	219,794,000	643,512,000	745,910,000	988,813,000)			...

General Population, Agriculture, and Manufacturing Statistics, 1790-1970

WEST VIRGINIA

Item No.	1790 (or 1789)	1800	1810	1820	1830	1840	1850	1860	1870*
1. Population[1, 50]	55,873[a]	78,592[a]	105,469[a]	136,808[a]	176,924[a]	224,537[a]	302,313[a]	376,688[a]	442,014
2. Decennial rates of increase in population over preceding census[2, 50]	...	40.7[a]	34.2[a]	29.7[a]	29.3[a]	26.9[a]	34.6[a]	24.6[a]	17.3
3. Increase in population over previous census[1, 3, 50]	...	22,719[a]	26,877[a]	31,339[a]	40,116[a]	47,613[a]	77,776[a]	74,375[a]	65,326
4. Percent distribution of population[4]	1.4[a]	1.5[a]	1.5[a]	1.4[a]	1.4[a]	1.3[a]	1.3[a]	1.2[a]	1.1
5. Population per square mile of land area[5, 6, 50]	...	...	...	...	...	...	...	...	18.4
6. Membership of House of Representatives at each apportionment[7]	...	...	...	...	...	...	...	...	3
7. White population[8, 9, 10, 51]	...	...	...	...	...	...	...	...	424,033
8. Percentage increase in white population over preceding census[9, 10, 11, 51]	...	...	...	...	...	...	...	...	...
9. Negro population[8, 9, 10, 51]	...	...	...	...	...	...	...	...	17,980
10. Percentage increase in Negro population over preceding census[9, 10, 11, 12, 13, 51]	...	...	...	...	...	...	...	...	...
11. Number of slaves in the area enumerated in 1790 and in the added area[14]	4,668[a]	7,172[a]	10,836[a]	15,119[a]	17,673[a]	18,488[a]	20,500[a]	18,371[a]	...
12. Urban population[15, 50]	...	...	...	...	...	7,885[a]	11,435[a]	20,077[a]	36,009
13. Percent urban increase over preceding census[15, 50]	...	...	...	...	...	...	45.0	75.6	79.4
14. Rural population[15, 50]	55,873[a]	78,592[a]	105,469[a]	136,808[a]	176,924[a]	216,652[a]	290,878[a]	356,611[a]	406,005
15. Percent rural increase over preceding census[15, 50]	...	40.7	34.2	29.7	29.3	22.5	34.3	22.6	13.9
16. Percent of urban to total population[15, 50]	...	...	...	...	...	3.5	3.8	5.3	8.1
17. Percent of rural to total population[15, 50]	100.0	100.0	100.0	100.0	100.0	96.5	96.2	94.7	91.9
18. Number of farms[16, 52]	...	...	...	...	...	...	...	...	39,778
19. Acres in farms[16, 52]	...	...	...	...	...	...	...	...	8,528,394
20. Acres improved land in farms[17]	...	...	...	...	...	...	...	...	2,580,254
21. Cropland harvested, acres[16, 53]	...	...	...	...	...	...	...	...	...
22. Percentage increase in farm population[17, 18]	...	...	...	...	...	...	...	...	...
23. Percentage increase in number of farms[16, 17]	...	...	...	...	...	...	...	...	...
24. Percentage increase of land in farms[16, 17]	...	...	...	...	...	...	...	...	...
25. Percentage increase of improved land in farms[17]	...	...	...	...	...	...	...	...	...

WEST VIRGINIA

1880	1890	1900	1910	1920	1930	1940	1950	1960	1970
618,457	762,794	958,800	1,221,119	1,463,701	1,729,205	1,901,974	2,005,552	1,860,421	1,744,237
39.9	23.3	25.7	27.4	19.9	18.1	10.0	5.4	-7.2	-6.2
176,443	144,337	196,006	262,319	252,582	265,504	172,769	103,578	-145,131	-116,184
1.2	1.2	1.3	1.3	1.4	1.4	1.4	1.3	1.0	...
25.7	31.8	39.9	50.8	60.9	71.8	79.0	83.3	77.3	72.5
4	4	5	6	6	6	6	6	5	4
592,537	730,077	915,233	1,156,817	1,377,235	1,614,191	1,784,102	1,890,282	1,770,133	1,673,480
39.7	23.2	25.4	26.4	19.1	17.2	10.5	5.9	-6.3	-5.5
25,886	32,690	43,499	64,173	86,345	114,893	117,754	114,867	89,378	67,342
44.0	26.3	33.1	47.5	34.6	33.1	2.5	-2.4	-22.2	-24.7
...	...	...	...	...	...	...	...	...	...
54,050	81,365	125,465	228,242	369,007	491,504	534,292	640,606[b] 694,487[c]	665,504[b] 711,101[c]	679,491
50.1	50.5	54.2	81.9	61.7	33.2	8.7	19.9[b] ...[c]	3.9[b] 2.4[c]	-4.5
564,407	681,429	833,335	992,877	1,094,694	1,237,701	1,367,682	1,364,946[b] 1,311,065[c]	1,194,917[b] 1,149,320[c]	1,064,746
39.0	20.7	22.3	19.1	10.3	13.1	10.5	-0.2[b] ...[c]	-12.5[b] -12.3[c]	-7.4
8.7	10.7	13.1	18.7	25.2	28.4	28.1	31.9[b] 34.6[c]	35.8[b] 38.2[c]	39.0
91.3	89.3	86.9	81.3	74.8	71.6	71.9	68.1[b] 65.4[c]	64.2[b] 61.8[c]	61.0
62,674	72,773	92,874	96,685	87,289	82,641	99,282	81,434	44,011[d]	29,000
10,193,779	10,321,326	10,654,513	10,026,442	9,569,790	8,802,348	8,908,803	8,214,626	6,062,594[d]	5,100,000
3,792,327	4,554,000	5,498,981	5,521,757	5,520,308	...	...	...	...	...
1,506,407	1,771,976	1,992,403	1,874,382	1,891,515	1,655,380	1,564,754	1,218,239	831,884[d]	722,000
39.9	23.3	25.7	27.4	19.9	-6.0	...	...	...	...
57.6	16.1	27.6	4.1	-9.7	-5.3	20.1	-18.0	-45.9[d]	...
19.5	1.3	3.2	-5.9	-4.6	-8.0	1.2	-7.8	-26.2[d]	...
47.0	20.1	20.8	0.4	...	...	...	...	...	...

Item No.	1790 (or 1789)	1800	1810	1820	1830	1840	1850	1860	1870*
26. Average acreage per farm[16]	...	...	...	...	...	...	...	...	214.4
27. Percentage increase in cropland harvested[16]	...	...	...	...	...	...	...	...	...
28. Value of farms, dollars[16]	...	...	...	...	...	...	...	...	81,283,505
29. Value of farms, percent increase[16]	...	...	...	...	...	...	...	...	...
30. Average value per farm, dollars[16]	...	...	...	...	...	...	...	...	2,043
31. Farms operated by owners[19, 20, 21, 22, 23, 24]	...	...	...	...	...	...	...	...	...
32. Value of livestock on farms, dollars[25, 26, 27, 54]	...	...	...	...	...	...	...	...	13,740,336[g]
33. Average value of livestock per farm, dollars[25, 26, 27, 52, 54]	...	...	...	...	...	...	...	...	345[g]
34. Production of cotton in commercial bales[28, 29, 30, 31]	...	...	...	...	...	...	...	...	...
35. Percent of total production of cotton[28, 29, 30, 31]	...	...	...	...	...	...	...	...	...
36. Production of corn in bushels[32, 33, 34, 35, 53]	...	...	...	...	...	...	...	...	8,197,865
37. Percent of total production of corn[32, 33, 34, 35, 53]	...	...	...	...	...	...	...	...	1.1
38. Production of tobacco in pounds[36, 37, 38, 53]	...	...	...	...	...	...	...	...	2,046,452
39. Percent of total production of tobacco[36, 37, 38, 53]	...	...	...	...	...	...	...	...	0.8
40. Production of rice in pounds[39]	...	...	...	...	...	...	...	...	...
41. Production of rice in bushels[40, 41]	...	...	...	...	...	...	...	...	...
42. Percent of total production of rice[39, 40, 41]	...	...	...	...	...	...	...	...	...
43. Number of manufacturing establishments[42, 43, 44, 45, 46, 55]	...	...	...	...	...	...	...	...	2,444
44. Capital of manufacturing establishments[42, 43, 44]	...	...	...	...	...	...	...	...	11,084,520
45. Average number of wage earners[42, 43, 44, 45, 46, 55]	...	...	...	...	...	...	...	...	11,672
46. Total wages[42, 43, 45, 46, 55]	...	...	...	...	...	...	...	...	4,322,164
47. Cost of materials used in manufacturing[42, 43, 44, 45, 46, 55]	...	...	...	...	...	...	...	...	14,503,701
48. Value of manufactured product[42, 43, 44, 45, 46]	...	...	...	...	...	...	...	...	24,102,201

a. Population of region now comprising West Virginia

b. Previous urban/rural definition. Rural included population residing outside of incorporated places having 2,500 inhabitants or more.

c. Current urban/rural definition. Urban includes those residing in urban/fringe areas and in unincorporated places of 2,500 or more.

d. For 1959

e. Based on a sampling of farms

f. Includes part owners

g. Values in gold

h. For 1967

*The 1970 Census of population is considered incomplete in the Southern states.

1880	1890	1900	1910	1920	1930	1940	1950	1960	1970
162.6	141.8	114.7	103.7	109.6	106.5	89.7	100.9	137.8[d]	. . .
. . .	17.6	12.4	-5.9	0.9	-12.5	-5.5	-22.1	-31.7[d]	. . .
133,147,175	151,880,300	168,295,670	264,390,954	410,783,406	341,976,394	269,827,285	487,209,000[e]	450,246,000[d, e]	. . .
63.8	14.1	10.8	57.1	55.4	-16.7	-21.1	80.6[e]	-7.6[d, e]	. . .
2,124	2,087	1,812	2,735	4,706	4,138	2,718	5,983[e]	10,230[d, e]	. . .
50,673	59,858	72,583	75,978[f]	72,101[f]	66,573[f]	76,325[f]	72,863[f]	40,956[d, f]	. . .
17,742,387	23,964,610	30,571,259	43,336,073	66,684,095	54,070,701	36,515,689	80,663,228	78,018,091[d]	84,141,000
283	329	329	448	771	654	368	991	1,773[d]	2,901
. . .	. . .	. . .	. . .	. . .	. . .	. . .	. . .	. . .	. . .
. . .	. . .	. . .	. . .	. . .	. . .	. . .	. . .	. . .	. . .
14,090,609	13,730,506	16,610,730	17,119,097	17,010,357	11,656,200	12,391,025	9,659,976	7,650,000	3,120,000
0.8	0.6	0.6	0.7	0.7	0.5	0.5	0.3	0.2	0.1
2,296,146	2,602,021	3,087,140	14,356,400	7,587,052	5,361,698	2,165,779	3,755,502	2,975,626	3,256,000
0.5	0.5	0.4	1.3	0.5	0.4	0.1	0.2	0.2	0.2
. . .	. . .	. . .	. . .	. . .	. . .	. . .	. . .	. . .	. . .
. . .	. . .	. . .	. . .	. . .	. . .	. . .	. . .	. . .	. . .
. . .	. . .	. . .	. . .	. . .	. . .	. . .	. . .	. . .	. . .
2,375	2,376	4,418	2,586	2,785	1,488	1,130)			1,844[h]
13,883,390	28,118,030	55,904,238	150,922,000	339,190,000	. . .	. . .)			. . .
14,311	19,340	33,272	63,893	83,036	85,326	74,989)	See following table		124,000[h]
4,313,965	6,911,779	12,969,237	33,000,000	101,840,000	115,295,000	88,487,000)			831,600,000[h]
14,027,388	23,729,089	43,006,880	92,878,000	270,941,000	261,398,000	227,062,000)			1,899,800,000[h]
22,867,126	38,702,125	74,838,330	161,949,000	471,971,000	513,012,000	441,840,000)			. . .

General Statistics for Manufacturing Establishments by State[47]

	1899	1909	1919	1929	1939	1947	1954	1958	1963
ALABAMA									
1. Total establishments (number)	2,000	3,398	3,522	2,848	1,982	3,336	3,893	3,956	4,079
2. With 20 employees or more	(NA)	(NA)	(NA)	(NA)	(NA)	(NA)	1,152	1,195	1,257
3. All employees, total (number)	54,970	78,203	116,440	130,034	129,261	206,239	220,077	229,830	243,800
4. Payroll ($1,000)	16,971	33,849	116,974	126,390	114,706	444,887	690,015	920,009	1,162,409
5. Production workers, total (number)	52,711	72,148	106,679	119,559	115,698	185,700	188,414	188,743	197,646
6. Man-hours (1,000)	(NA)	(NA)	(NA)	(NA)	(NA)	(NA)	357,780	363,169	390,979
7. Wages ($1,000)	14,912	27,284	98,482	102,005	91,106	372,510	528,618	677,598	842,277
8. Value added by manufacture, adjusted ($1,000)	34,112	62,519	190,965	258,125	245,577	877,416	1,319,192	1,770,510	2,515,011
9. Capital expenditures, new ($1,000)	(NA)	(NA)	(NA)	(NA)	(NA)	(NA)	82,248	165,144	147,395
10. Percent of U. S. employment	1.13	1.12	1.18	1.35	1.36	1.44	1.37	1.43	1.44
11. Index of employment change (1958 = 100)	25	36	54	60	60	95	96	100	106
12. U. S. index of employment change (1958 = 100)	31	45	63	62	61	91	100	100	106
ARKANSAS									
1. Total establishments (number)	1,746	2,925	3,044	1,731	1,115	1,926	2,428	2,589	2,859
2. With 20 employees or more	(NA)	(NA)	(NA)	(NA)	(NA)	(NA)	568	666	840
3. All employees, total (number)	33,074	48,275	54,234	48,747	41,183	65,802	79,052	88,724	113,658
4. Payroll ($1,000)	11,447	22,574	56,207	49,446	33,352	125,200	221,763	293,043	439,572
5. Production workers, total (number)	31,525	44,982	49,693	44,205	35,672	58,725	67,481	74,429	95,551
6. Man-hours (1,000)	(NA)	(NA)	(NA)	(NA)	(NA)	(NA)	134,479	144,699	191,828
7. Wages ($1,000)	10,184	19,113	46,909	39,503	24,205	102,838	171,109	220,862	331,715
8. Value added by manufacture, adjusted ($1,000)	21,600	39,981	96,953	94,255	66,444	267,516	457,047	591,745	960,886
9. Capital expenditures, new ($1,000)	(NA)	(NA)	(NA)	(NA)	(NA)	(NA)	42,715	48,227	73,383
10. Percent of U. S. employment	0.68	0.69	0.55	0.50	0.43	0.46	0.49	0.55	0.67
11. Index of employment change (1958 = 100)	37	54	61	55	46	74	89	100	128
12. U. S. index of employment change (1958 = 100)	30	44	61	60	59	89	100	100	106

General Statistics for Manufacturing Establishments by State[47]

	1899	1909	1919	1929	1939	1947	1954	1958	1963
DELAWARE									
1. Total establishments (number)	633	726	653	460	416	483	556	569	569
2. With 20 employees or more	(NA)	(NA)	(NA)	(NA)	(NA)	(NA)	209	222	243
3. All employees, total (number)	21,751	23,262	33,231	26,556	23,360	34,738	54,530	57,830	58,395
4. Payroll ($1,000)	9,794	12,618	44,914	37,407	29,114	92,858	267,354	347,603	429,626
5. Production workers, total (number)	20,562	21,238	28,994	23,552	19,825	29,275	30,988	29,966	30,417
6. Man-hours (1,000)	(NA)	(NA)	(NA)	(NA)	(NA)	(NA)	60,451	57,283	61,487
7. Wages ($1,000)	8,457	10,296	37,214	29,063	21,163	70,578	104,882	125,244	159,025
8. Value added by manufacture, adjusted ($1,000)	16,596	21,902	79,547	69,151	54,085	183,073	353,083	419,831	658,189
9. Capital expenditures, new ($1,000)	(NA)	(NA)	(NA)	(NA)	(NA)	(NA)	23,375	27,926	88,806
10. Percent of U. S. employment	0.45	0.33	0.34	0.27	0.25	0.24	0.34	0.36	0.34
11. Index of employment change (1958 = 100)	37	40	57	46	40	60	94	100	101
12. U. S. index of employment change (1958 = 100)	30	44	61	60	59	89	100	100	106
FLORIDA									
1. Total establishments (number)	1,275	2,159	2,503	2,212	1,976	2,807	4,792	6,349	7,377
2. With 20 employees or more	(NA)	(NA)	(NA)	(NA)	(NA)	755	1,065	1,526	1,826
3. All employees, total (number)	37,252	62,098	80,086	71,345	62,616	78,665	123,944	171,251	215,447
4. Payroll ($1,000)	12,216	27,937	77,932	66,651	55,355	168,817	389,284	680,521	1,102,283
5. Production workers, total (number)	35,471	57,473	74,156	64,868	51,149	66,027	97,338	125,089	148,386
6. Man-hours (1,000)	(NA)	(NA)	(NA)	(NA)	(NA)	139,890	198,489	247,753	301,308
7. Wages ($1,000)	10,916	22,982	67,136	54,582	36,847	128,239	270,749	434,529	626,201
8. Value added by manufacture, adjusted ($1,000)	21,336	46,761	120,151	135,488	115,885	349,976	797,721	1,410,843	2,351,973
9. Capital expenditures, new ($1,000)	(NA)	(NA)	(NA)	(NA)	(NA)	50,052	104,631	152,303	190,617
10. Percent of U. S. employment	0.77	0.89	0.81	0.74	0.66	0.55	0.77	1.07	1.27
11. Index of employment change (1958 = 100)	22	36	47	42	37	46	72	100	126
12. U. S. index of employment change (1958 = 100)	30	44	61	60	59	89	100	100	106

	1899	1909	1919	1929	1939	1947	1954	1958	1963
GEORGIA									
1. Total establishments (number)	3,015	4,792	4,608	4,179	3,055	4,755	5,655	5,860	6,249
2. With 20 employees or more	(NA)	(NA)	(NA)	(NA)	(NA)	(NA)	1,713	1,844	2,056
3. All employees, total (number)	87,151	112,895	135,263	171,734	176,965	249,958	303,017	314,088	354,023
4. Payroll ($1,000)	23,162	43,867	125,503	140,674	142,021	484,289	853,496	1,074,972	1,505,556
5. Production workers, total (number)	83,336	104,588	122,578	158,774	155,870	225,838	260,082	261,099	290,008
6. Man-hours (1,000)	(NA)	(NA)	(NA)	(NA)	(NA)	(NA)	503,497	500,334	582,382
7. Wages ($1,000)	19,958	34,805	100,146	110,435	106,195	399,862	642,582	775,947	1,073,001
8. Value added by manufacture, adjusted ($1,000)	45,176	85,893	251,098	294,649	280,032	1,016,079	1,592,411	2,102,332	3,254,007
9. Capital expenditures, new ($1,000)	(NA)	(NA)	(NA)	(NA)	(NA)	(NA)	162,849	169,871	202,163
10. Percent of U. S. employment	1.80	1.61	1.38	1.78	1.86	1.75	1.88	1.96	2.09
11. Index of employment change (1958 = 100)	28	36	43	55	56	80	96	100	113
12. U. S. index of employment change (1958 = 100)	30	44	61	60	39	89	100	100	106
KENTUCKY									
1. Total establishments (number)	3,648	4,776	3,767	2,246	1,582	2,245	2,651	2,903	2,946
2. With 20 employees or more	(NA)	(NA)	(NA)	(NA)	(NA)	(NA)	851	927	1,025
3. All employees, total (number)	56,091	74,010	79,261	88,583	76,504	129,553	151,113	162,243	180,460
4. Payroll ($1,000)	22,639	37,491	85,845	113,623	89,004	304,782	553,203	721,421	959,001
5. Production workers, total (number)	51,735	65,400	68,726	77,825	62,481	110,648	119,218	124,704	140,536
6. Man-hours (1,000)	(NA)	(NA)	(NA)	(NA)	(NA)	(NA)	233,719	241,746	280,442
7. Wages ($1,000)	18,454	27,888	66,261	88,644	61,592	236,085	383,945	491,809	657,409
8. Value added by manufacture, adjusted ($1,000)	59,102	111,975	158,498	236,080	186,485	743,322	1,236,260	1,769,269	2,548,531
9. Capital expenditures, new ($1,000)	(NA)	(NA)	(NA)	(NA)	(NA)	(NA)	124,037	112,525	223,561
10. Percent of U. S. employment	1.16	1.06	0.81	0.92	0.82	0.91	0.94	1.01	1.06
11. Index of employment change (1958 = 100)	35	46	49	55	47	80	93	100	111
12. U. S. index of employment change (1958 = 100)	30	44	61	60	59	89	100	100	106

General Statistics for Manufacturing Establishments by State [47]

	1899	1909	1919	1929	1939	1947	1954	1958	1963
LOUISIANA									
1. Total establishments (number)	1,826	2,516	2,489	1,989	1,779	2,388	3,020	3,156	3,222
2. With 20 employees or more	(NA)	(NA)	(NA)	(NA)	(NA)	949	897	935	954
3. All employees, total (number)	44,454	84,268	109,853	97,551	87,770	132,463	145,250	136,944	139,511
4. Payroll ($1,000)	17,659	42,394	116,718	107,960	85,273	309,869	533,947	621,397	769,410
5. Production workers, total (number)	40,878	76,165	97,742	87,345	70,453	111,552	114,378	103,519	104,720
6. Man-hours (1,000)	(NA)	(NA)	(NA)	(NA)	(NA)	231,384	232,019	205,887	215,445
7. Wages ($1,000)	14,725	33,386	93,858	83,867	54,454	229,671	375,730	426,345	526,177
8. Value added by manufacture, adjusted ($1,000)	35,994	89,084	243,886	246,497	198,527	694,062	1,181,649	1,429,580	1,915,625
9. Capital expenditures, new ($1,000)	(NA)	(NA)	(NA)	(NA)	(NA)	97,210	174,396	173,383	210,837
10. Percent of U. S. employment	0.92	1.20	1.12	1.01	0.92	0.93	0.90	0.85	0.82
11. Index of employment change (1958 = 100)	32	62	80	71	64	97	106	100	102
12. U. S. index of employment change (1958 = 100)	30	44	61	60	59	89	100	100	106
MARYLAND									
1. Total establishments (number)	3,886	4,837	4,725	3,231	2,712	2,826	3,253	3,435	3,519
2. With 20 employees or more	(NA)	(NA)	(NA)	(NA)	(NA)	(NA)	1,279	1,334	1,394
3. All employees, total (number)	100,911	120,113	159,362	150,906	166,091	228,655	255,447	259,097	263,672
4. Payroll ($1,000)	39,260	59,053	188,223	195,013	209,193	612,296	1,002,037	1,257,423	1,549,834
5. Production workers, total (number)	94,170	107,921	139,241	131,099	140,930	188,696	195,916	190,472	188,876
6. Man-hours (1,000)	(NA)	(NA)	(NA)	(NA)	(NA)	(NA)	384,180	368,548	375,863
7. Wages ($1,000)	32,414	45,436	146,578	148,835	155,938	458,282	675,056	813,332	960,491
8. Value added by manufacture, adjusted ($1,000)	81,722	116,620	322,092	422,097	420,589	1,139,240	1,888,585	2,394,414	3,001,468
9. Capital expenditures, new ($1,000)	(NA)	(NA)	(NA)	(NA)	(NA)	(NA)	93,908	128,085	176,307
10. Percent of U. S. employment	2.08	1.71	1.62	1.56	1.74	1.60	1.59	1.62	1.55
11. Index of employment change (1958 = 100)	39	46	62	58	64	88	99	100	102
12. U. S. index of employment change (1958 = 100)	30	44	61	60	59	89	100	100	106

General Statistics for Manufacturing Establishments by State [47]

	1899	1909	1919	1929	1939	1947	1954	1958	1963
MISSISSIPPI									
1. Total establishments (number)	1,294	2,598	2,379	1,911	1,235	1,985	2,252	2,433	2,384
2. With 20 employees or more	(NA)	(NA)	(NA)	(NA)	(NA)	(NA)	665	743	848
3. All employees, total (number)	28,059	53,787	61,452	56,268	52,064	77,353	90,852	108,539	128,506
4. Payroll ($1,000)	9,003	22,422	58,959	51,427	36,498	138,970	238,681	354,414	486,210
5. Production workers, total (number)	26,799	50,384	57,383	52,086	45,893	70,282	79,834	92,468	108,480
6. Man-hours (1,000)	(NA)	(NA)	(NA)	(NA)	(NA)	(NA)	156,930	178,705	214,503
7. Wages ($1,000)	7,910	18,768	51,040	42,208	27,130	116,242	188,803	280,849	367,921
8. Value added by manufacture, adjusted ($1,000)	17,175	43,630	100,559	107,325	72,661	302,268	467,625	642,175	1,016,962
9. Capital expenditures, new ($1,000)	(NA)	(NA)	(NA)	(NA)	(NA)	(NA)	37,008	67,665	131,201
10. Percent of U. S. employment	0.58	0.77	0.62	0.58	0.55	0.54	0.56	0.68	0.76
11. Index of employment change (1958 = 100)	26	50	57	52	48	71	84	100	118
12. U. S. index of employment change (1958 = 100)	30	44	61	60	59	89	100	100	106
NORTH CAROLINA									
1. Total establishments (number)	3,465	4,931	5,690	3,797	3,158	5,321	6,645	7,352	7,784
2. With 20 employees or more	(NA)	(NA)	(NA)	(NA)	(NA)	(NA)	2,369	2,628	2,946
3. All employees, total (number)	75,216	128,002	167,848	226,425	293,258	381,438	434,934	461,485	530,646
4. Payroll ($1,000)	16,447	41,259	148,361	198,810	245,879	758,757	1,185,629	1,488,645	2,092,075
5. Production workers, total (number)	72,322	121,473	156,376	209,826	269,238	350,177	380,089	391,712	444,400
6. Man-hours (1,000)	(NA)	(NA)	(NA)	(NA)	(NA)	(NA)	719,429	747,353	890,230
7. Wages ($1,000)	14,052	34,355	124,978	160,868	198,519	641,917	915,683	1,109,707	1,527,481
8. Value added by manufacture, adjusted ($1,000)	40,420	94,795	413,707	693,013	544,181	1,646,030	2,210,463	3,077,929	4,566,547
9. Capital expenditures, new ($1,000)	(NA)	(NA)	(NA)	(NA)	(NA)	(NA)	129,622	182,005	314,428
10. Percent of U. S. employment	1.55	1.83	1.70	2.34	3.08	2.67	2.70	2.88	3.13
11. Index of employment change (1958 = 100)	16	28	36	49	63	83	93	100	115
12. U. S. index of employment change (1958 = 100)	30	44	61	60	59	89	100	100	106

General Statistics for Manufacturing Establishments by State [47]

	1899	1909	1919	1929	1939	1947	1954	1958	1963
OKLAHOMA									
1. Total establishments (number)	495	2,310	2,316	1,658	1,530	1,740	2,131	2,409	2,575
2. With 20 employees or more	(NA)	(NA)	(NA)	(NA)	(NA)	(NA)	524	572	648
3. All employees, total (number)	2,650	15,336	35,445	38,638	37,585	55,441	89,257	91,587	97,691
4. Payroll ($1,000)	1,113	9,285	46,234	57,604	47,170	143,634	363,627	446,358	551,677
5. Production workers, total (number)	2,381	13,143	29,048	31,695	27,642	44,349	60,572	59,739	64,195
6. Man-hours (1,000)	(NA)	(NA)	(NA)	(NA)	(NA)	(NA)	122,530	118,407	130,085
7. Wages ($1,000)	894	7,240	34,423	41,277	29,957	105,327	212,183	248,548	294,968
8. Value added by manufacture, adjusted ($1,000)	2,703	19,530	87,551	149,404	101,782	341,149	580,633	724,998	978,774
9. Capital expenditures, new ($1,000)	(NA)	(NA)	(NA)	(NA)	(NA)	(NA)	51,740	61,927	63,562
10. Percent of U. S. employment	0.05	0.22	0.36	0.40	0.40	0.39	0.55	0.57	0.58
11. Index of employment change (1958 = 100)	2	16	38	42	41	61	97	100	106
12. U. S. index of employment change (1958 = 100)	30	44	61	60	59	89	100	107	106
SOUTH CAROLINA									
1. Total establishments (number)	1,369	1,854	1,821	1,659	1,300	2,135	2,720	2,911	3,057
2. With 20 employees or more	(NA)	(NA)	(NA)	(NA)	(NA)	(NA)	834	939	1,076
3. All employees, total (number)	48,444	76,303	83,982	113,876	136,094	188,760	219,923	225,51u	261,655
4. Payroll ($1,000)	10,438	24,117	72,336	86,023	103,171	377,105	634,756	732,149	1,046,514
5. Production workers, total (number)	47,025	73,046	78,918	108,777	126,408	175,889	190,119	193,936	221,198
6. Man-hours (1,000)	(NA)	(NA)	(NA)	(NA)	(NA)	(NA)	378,931	381,540	453,962
7. Wages ($1,000)	9,130	20,361	61,934	73,223	86,280	330,670	486,960	565,014	790,954
8. Value added by manufacture, adjusted ($1,000)	22,850	46,885	152,301	159,351	169,294	793,915	1,040,936	1,360,135	2,111,117
9. Capital expenditures, new ($1,000)	(NA)	(NA)	(NA)	(NA)	(NA)	(NA)	59,629	75,617	179,264
10. Percent of U. S. employment	1.00	1.09	0.85	1.18	1.43	1.32	1.37	1.41	1.54
11. Index of employment change (1958 = 100)	21	34	37	50	60	84	98	100	106
12. U. S. index of employment change (1958 = 100)	30	44	61	60	59	89	100	100	106

General Statistics for Manufacturing Establishments by State [47]

	1899	1909	1919	1929	1939	1947	1954	1958	1963
TENNESSEE									
1. Total establishments (number)	3,116	4,609	4,426	2,855	2,225	3,345	4,058	4,508	4,787
2. With 20 employees or more	(NA)	(NA)	(NA)	(NA)	(NA)	(NA)	1,366	1,516	1,809
3. All employees total (number)	49,292	82,257	107,725	142,020	152,179	222,300	267,496	282,862	339,108
4. Payroll ($1,000)	17,775	37,438	105,861	149,080	149,525	474,978	882,644	1,103,409	1,542,227
5. Production workers, total (number)	45,963	73,840	94,564	128,400	131,024	193,197	214,027	220,823	266,969
6. Man-hours (1,000)	(NA)	(NA)	(NA)	(NA)	(NA)	(NA)	418,378	426,647	530,222
7. Wages ($1,000)	14,728	28,252	80,687	115,877	108,828	371,637	612,461	739,504	1,040,681
8. Value added by manufacture, adjusted ($1,000)	38,190	76,201	210,201	322,898	318,378	961,385	1,678,786	2,207,073	3,302,688
9. Capital expenditures, new ($1,000)	(NA)	(NA)	(NA)	(NA)	(NA)	(NA)	152,698	209,712	244,897
10. Percent of U. S. employment	1.02	1.17	1.10	1.47	1.60	1.56	1.66	1.76	2.00
11. Index of employment change (1958 = 100)	17	29	38	50	54	79	95	100	120
12. U. S. index of employment change (1958 = 100)	30	44	61	60	59	89	100	100	106
TEXAS									
1. Total establishments (number)	3,107	4,588	5,390	5,198	5,085	7,129	8,890	10,505	11,581
2. With 20 employees or more	(NA)	(NA)	(NA)	(NA)	(NA)	(NA)	2,612	3,088	3,478
3. All employees total (number)	41,465	80,079	124,110	156,143	163,978	297,054	417,210	477,591	513,802
4. Payroll ($1,000)	19,830	48,775	146,230	201,732	196,747	755,413	1,659,263	2,284,871	2,890,778
5. Production workers, total (number)	38,604	70,230	106,268	134,498	125,115	242,015	313,938	343,092	361,471
6. Man-hours (1,000)	(NA)	(NA)	(NA)	(NA)	(NA)	(NA)	639,565	683,081	742,551
7. Wages ($1,000)	16,912	37,907	114,935	151,827	126,364	558,422	1,109,061	1,453,915	1,744,187
8. Value added by manufacture, adjusted ($1,000)	38,506	94,717	295,709	460,307	448,523	1,727,476	3,501,706	5,045,159	7,086,283
9. Capital expenditures, new ($1,000)	(NA)	(NA)	(NA)	(NA)	(NA)	(NA)	452,214	640,516	567,264
10. Percent of U. S. employment	0.85	1.14	1.26	1.62	1.72	2.08	2.59	2.98	3.03
11. Index of employment change (1958 = 100)	9	17	26	33	34	62	87	100	108
12. U. S. index of employment change (1958 = 100)	30	44	61	60	59	89	100	100	106

	1899	1909	1919	1929	1939	1947	1954	1958	1963
VIRGINIA									
1. Total establishments (number)	3,186	5,867	5,487	3,287	2,494	3,643	4,398	4,472	4,542
2. With 20 employees or more	(NA)	(NA)	(NA)	(NA)	(NA)	(NA)	1,290	1,381	1,573
3. All employees total (number)	70,051	114,227	132,842	131,586	150,202	216,507	242,768	258,136	302,084
4. Payroll ($1,000)	23,903	47,256	145,423	147,352	150,359	483,575	776,820	986,545	1,431,977
5. Production workers, total (number)	66,223	105,676	118,976	120,273	132,089	189,942	202,654	204,357	239,631
6. Man-hours (1,000)	(NA)	(NA)	(NA)	(NA)	(NA)	(NA)	394,735	397,567	480,228
7. Wages ($1,000)	20,274	38,155	119,583	118,089	113,848	384,293	576,844	686,814	992,099
8. Value added by manufacture, adjusted ($1,000)	49,285	94,211	271,131	380,086	376,259	1,050,623	1,629,041	2,122,652	3,046,268
9. Capital expenditures, new ($1,000)	(NA)	(NA)	(NA)	(NA)	(NA)	(NA)	109,887	146,463	231,786
10. Percent of U. S. employment	1.44	1.63	1.35	1.36	1.58	1.51	1.51	1.61	1.78
11. Index of employment change (1958 = 100)	27	44	51	51	58	84	94	100	117
12. U. S. index of employment change (1958 = 100)	30	44	61	60	59	89	100	100	106
WEST VIRGINIA									
1. Total establishments (number)	1,824	2,586	2,627	1,488	1,094	1,602	2,027	1,916	1,832
2. With 20 employees or more	(NA)	(NA)	(NA)	(NA)	(NA)	558	517	519	528
3. All employees total (number)	34,824	68,864	90,651	93,565	87,741	127,354	122,390	116,201	117,026
4. Payroll ($1,000)	14,519	38,710	118,898	136,291	113,660	337,869	494,893	573,837	700,058
5. Production workers, total (number)	33,080	63,893	82,615	85,326	74,411	108,985	97,322	90,390	90,196
6. Man-hours (1,000)	(NA)	(NA)	(NA)	(NA)	(NA)	215,639	185,651	173,129	179,785
7. Wages ($1,000)	12,640	33,000	101,310	115,295	87,760	268,469	354,666	411,007	491,275
8. Value added by manufacture, adjusted ($1,000)	29,779	69,072	199,568	251,615	213,284	663,903	988,274	1,268,842	1,887,148
9. Capital expenditures, new ($1,000)	(NA)	(NA)	(NA)	(NA)	(NA)	82,332	98,883	171,937	173,002
10. Percent of U. S. employment	0.72	0.98	0.92	0.97	0.92	0.89	0.76	0.72	0.69
11. Index of employment change (1958 = 100)	30	59	78	81	76	110	105	100	101
12. U. S. index of employment change (1958 = 100)	30	44	61	60	59	89	100	100	106

Population of Cities Having 50,000 Inhabitants or More in 1950

1900 to 1970 [48, 49, 50]

	1900	1910	1920	1930	1940	1950	1960	1970[50]
Alexandria, Va.	14,528	15,329	18,060	13,139	22,412	61,787	91,023	110,938
Amarillo, Tex.	1,442	9,957	15,494	43,132	51,686	74,246	137,969	127,010
Asheville, N. C.	14,694	18,762	28,504	50,193	51,310	53,000	60,192	57,681
Atlanta, Ga.	89,872	154,839	200,616	270,366	302,288	331,314	487,455	496,973
Augusta, Ga.	39,441	41,040	52,548	60,342	65,919	71,508	70,626	59,864
Austin, Tex.	22,258	29,860	34,876	53,120	87,930	132,459	186,545	251,808
Baltimore, Md.	508,957	558,485	733,826	804,874	859,100	949,708	939,024	905,759
Baton Rouge, La.	11,269	14,897	21,782	30,729	34,719	125,629	152,419	165,963
Beaumont, Tex.	9,427	20,640	40,422	57,732	59,061	94,014	119,175	115,919
Birmingham, Ala.	38,415	132,685	178,806	259,678	267,583	326,037	340,887	300,910
Charleston, S. C.	55,807	58,833	67,957	62,265	71,275	70,174	65,925	66,945
Charleston, W. Va.	11,099	22,996	39,608	60,408	67,914	73,501	85,796	71,505
Charlotte, N. C.	18,091	34,014	46,338	82,675	100,899	134,042	201,564	241,178
Chattanooga, Tenn.	30,154	44,604	57,895	119,798	128,163	131,041	130,009	119,082
Columbia, S. C.	21,108	26,319	37,524	51,581	62,396	86,914	97,433	113,542
Columbus, Ga.	17,614	20,554	31,125	43,131	53,280	79,611	116,779	154,168
Corpus Christi, Tex.	4,703	8,222	10,522	27,741	57,301	108,287	167,690	204,525
Covington, Ky.	42,938	53,270	57,121	65,252	62,018	64,452	60,376	52,535
Dallas Tex.	42,638	92,104	158,976	260,475	294,734	434,462	679,684	1,844,401
Durham, N. C.	6,679	18,241	21,719	52,037	60,195	71,311	78,302	95,438
El Paso, Tex.	15,906	39,279	77,560	102,421	96,810	130,485	276,687	322,261
Fort Worth, Tex.	26,688	73,312	106,482	163,447	177,662	278,778	356,268	393,476
Gadsden, Ala.	4,282	10,557	14,737	24,042	36,975	55,725	58,088	53,928
Galveston, Tex.	37,789	36,981	44,255	52,938	60,862	66,568	67,175	61,809
Greensboro, N. C.	10,035	15,895	19,861	53,569	59,319	74,389	119,574	144,076
Greenville, S. C.	11,860	15,741	23,127	29,154	34,734	58,161	66,188	61,208
Houston, Tex.	44,633	78,800	138,276	292,352	384,514	596,163	938,219	1,232,802

Population of Cities Having 50,000 Inhabitants or More in 1950 (Cont.)

1900 to 1970[48, 49, 50]

	1900	1910	1920	1930	1940	1950	1960	1970[50]
Huntington, W. Va.	11,923	31,161	50,177	75,572	78,836	86,353	83,627	74,315
Jackson, Miss.	7,816	21,262	22,817	48,282	62,107	98,271	144,422	153,968
Jacksonville, Fla.	28,429	57,699	91,558	129,549	173,065	204,517	201,030	528,865
Laredo, Tex.	13,429	**14,855**	22,710	32,618	39,274	51,910	60,678	69,024
Lexington, Ky.	26,369	35,099	41,534	45,736	49,304	55,534	62,810	108,137
Little Rock, Ark.	38,307	45,941	65,142	81,679	88,039	102,213	107,813	132,483
Louisville, Ky.	204,731	223,928	234,891	307,745	319,077	369,129	390,639	361,472
Lubbock, Tex.	...	1,938	4,051	20,520	31,853	71,747	128,691	149,101
Macon, Ga.	23,272	40,665	52,995	53,829	57,865	70,252	69,764	122,423
Memphis, Tenn.	102,320	131,105	162,351	253,143	292,942	396,000	497,524	623,540
Miami, Fla.	1,681	5,471	29,571	110,637	172,172	249,276	291,688	334,859
Mobile, Ala.	38,469	51,521	60,777	68,202	78,720	129,009	202,779	190,026
Montgomery, Ala.	30,346	38,136	43,464	66,079	78,084	106,525	134,393	133,386
Nashville, Tenn.	80,865	110,364	118,342	153,866	167,402	174,307	170,874	448,003
New Orleans, La.	287,104	339,075	387,219	458,762	494,537	570,445	627,525	593,471
Norfolk, Va.	46,624	67,452	115,777	129,710	144,332	213,513	305,872	307,951
Oklahoma City, Okla.	10,037	64,205	91,295	185,389	204,424	243,504	324,253	366,481
Orlando, Fla.	2,481	3,894	9,282	27,330	36,736	52,367	88,135	99,006
Port Arthur, Tex.	900	7,663	22,251	50,902	46,140	57,530	66,676	57,371
Portsmouth, Va.	17,427	33,190	54,387	45,704	50,745	80,039	114,773	110,963
Raleigh, N. C.	13,643	19,218	24,418	37,379	46,897	65,679	93,931	121,577
Richmond, Va.	85,050	127,628	171,667	182,929	193,042	230,310	219,958	249,621
Roanoke, Va.	21,495	34,874	50,842	69,206	69,287	91,921	97,110	92,115
St. Petersburg, Fla.	1,575	4,127	14,237	40,425	60,812	96,738	181,298	216,232
San Angelo, Tex.	...	10,321	10,050	25,308	25,802	52,093	58,815	63,884
San Antonio, Tex.	53,321	96,614	161,379	231,542	253,854	408,442	587,718	654,153
Savannah, Ga.	54,244	65,064	83,252	85,024	95,996	119,638	149,245	118,349

Population of Cities Having 50,000 Inhabitants or More in 1950 (Cont.)

1900 to 1970 [48, 49, 50]

	1900	1910	1920	1930	1940	1950	1960	1970[50]
Shreveport, La.	16,013	28,015	43,874	76,655	98,167	127,206	164,372	182,064
Tampa, Fla.	15,839	37,782	51,608	101,161	108,391	124,681	274,970	277,767
Tulsa, Okla.	1,390	18,182	72,075	141,258	142,157	182,740	261,685	331,638
Waco, Tex.	20,686	26,425	38,500	52,848	55,982	84,706	97,808	95,326
Wheeling, W. Va.	38,878	41,641	56,208	61,659	61,099	58,891	53,400	48,188
Wichita Falls, Tex.	2,480	8,200	40,079	43,690	45,112	68,042	101,724	97,564
Wilmington, Del.	76,508	87,411	110,168	106,597	112,504	110,356	95,827	80,386
Winston-Salem, N. C.	13,650	22,700	48,395	75,274	79,815	87,811	111,135	132,913

NOTES

1. U.S. Bureau of the Census. *U. S. Census of Population: 1960,* Volume 1, Part 1, pp. 1-16, 1-17.

2. U. S. Bureau of the Census. *U. S. Census of Population: 1960,* Volume 1, Part 1, p. 1-18.

3. U. S. Bureau of the Census. *Twelfth Census of the U. S.: 1900,* Volume 1, Part 1, pp. 4-5.

4. U. S. Bureau of the Census. *U. S. Census of Population: 1960,* Volume 1, Part 1, p. 1-19.

5. U. S. Bureau of the Census. *U. S. Census of Population: 1960,* Volume 1, Part 1, p. 1-20.

6. U. S. Bureau of the Census. *Statistical Abstract of the U. S.:* 1940, p. 7.

7. U. S. Bureau of the Census. *U. S. Census of Population: 1960,* Volume 1, Part 1, p. 1-21.

8. U. S. Bureau of the Census. *Negro Population 1790-1915,* pp. 44-45.

9. U. S. Bureau of the Census. *Statistical Abstract of the U. S.: 1942,* pp. 12-13.

10. U. S. Bureau of the Census. *Statistical Abstract of the U. S.: 1963,* p. 30.

11. U. S. Bureau of the Census. *Twelfth Census of the U. S.: 1900, Special Reports of the Census Office, Supplementary Analysis,* pp. 242-246.

12. U. S. Bureau of the Census. *Abstract of the Fourteenth Census of the U. S.: 1920,* p. 105.

13. U. S. Bureau of the Census. *Abstract of the Fifteenth Census of the U. S.: 1930,* p. 89.

14. U. S. Bureau of the Census. *A Century of Population Growth in the U. S. 1790-1900,* p. 133.

15. U. S. Bureau of the Census. *U. S. Census of the Population: 1960,* Volume 1, Part 1, pp. 1-32-1-36.

16. U. S. Bureau of the Census. *U. S. Census of Agriculture: 1959,* Volume II, *General Report, Statistics by Subject,* pp. 58-61.

17. U. S. Bureau of the Census. *Abstract of the Fourteenth Census of the U. S. 1920,* pp. 594-597.

18. U. S. Bureau of the Census. *Abstract of the Fifteenth Census: 1930,* p. 19.

19. U. S. Bureau of the Census. *Twelfth Census of the U. S. Taken in the Year 1900, Agriculture,* Part 1, pp. 688-689.

20. U. S. Bureau of the Census. *Abstract of the Fourteenth Census of the U. S.: 1920,* p. 630.

21. U. S. Bureau of the Census. *Statistical Abstract of the U. S.: 1940,* pp. 644-645.

22. U. S. Bureau of the Census. *Statistical Abstract of the U. S.: 1941,* pp. 682-683.

23. U. S. Bureau of the Census. *Statistical Abstract of the U. S.: 1960,* p. 628.

24. U. S. Bureau of the Census. *Statistical Abstract of the U. S.: 1962,* p. 619.

25. U. S. Bureau of the Census. *Twelfth Census of the United States Taken in the Year 1900,* Agriculture, Part 1, pp. 700-701.

26. U. S. Bureau of the Census. *Abstract of the Fourteenth Census of the U. S.: 1920,* pp. 752-753.

27. U. S. Bureau of the Census. *U. S. Census of Agriculture: 1959,* Volume II, *General Report, Statistics by Subject,* p. 497.

28. U. S. Bureau of the Census. *Twelfth Census of the United States Taken in the Year 1900, Agriculture,* Part II, p. 425.

29. U. S. Bureau of the Census. *Abstract of the Fourteenth Census of the U. S.: 1920,* p. 860.

30. U. S. Bureau of the Census. *U. S. Census of Agriculture: 1959,* Volume II, *General Report, Statistics by Subject,* p. 835.

31. U. S. Bureau of the Census, *U. S. Census of Agriculture: 1959,* Volume II, *General Report. Statistics by Subject,* p. 829.

32. U. S. Bureau of the Census. *Twelfth Census of the United States Taken in the Year 1900,* Volume VI, *Agriculture,* Part II, pp. 80-81.

33. U. S. Bureau of the Census. *Abstract of the Fourteenth Census of the U.S.: 1920,* p. 819.

34. U. S. Bureau of the Census. *U. S. Census of Agriculture: 1959,* Volume II, *General Report, Statistics by Subject,* pp. 706-707.

35. U. S. Bureau of the Census. *Statistical Abstract of the U. S.: 1961,* p. 658.

36. U. S. Bureau of the Census. *Twelfth Census of the United States Taken in the Year 1900, Agriculture,* Part 1, pp. 528-529.

NOTES (Cont.)

37. U. S. Bureau of the Census. *U. S. Census of Agriculture: 1959,* Volume II *General Report, Statistics by Subject,* pp. 840-841.

38. U. S. Bureau of the Census. *U. S. Census of Agriculture: 1959,* Volume II, *General Report, Statistics by Subject,* p. 836.

39. U. S. Bureau of the Census. *Twelfth Census of the United States Taken in the Year 1900,* Volume VI, *Agriculture,* Part II, p. 94.

40. U. S. Bureau of the Census. *U. S. Census of Agriculture: 1959,* Volume II, *General Report, Statistics by Subject,* p. 760.

41. U. S. Bureau of the Census. *U. S. Census of Agriculture: 1959,* Volume II, *General Report, Statistics by Subject,* p. 761.

42. U. S. Bureau of the Census. *Twelfth Census of the United States Taken in the Year 1900,* Volume VIII, Part II, pp. 982-989.

43. U. S. Bureau of the Census. *Abstract of the Fourteenth Census of the U. S.: 1920, pp. 1170-1171.*

44. U. S. Bureau of the Census. *Abstract of the Fourteenth Census of the U. S.: 1920,* p. 920.

45. U. S. Bureau of the Census. *Statistical Abstract of the U. S.: 1941,* pp. 758-759.

46. U. S. Bureau of the Census. *Statistical Abstract of the U. S.: 1941,* p. 880.

47. U. S. Bureau of the Census. *1963 Census of Manufactures,* Volume I, Summary and Subject Statistics, pp. 86-92.

48. U. S. Bureau of the Census. *Statistical Abstract of the U. S.: 1960,* pp. 18-21.

49. U. S. Bureau of the Census. *County and City Data Book: 1962.*

50. U. S. Bureau of the Census. U. S. Census of Population: 1970. *Number of Inhabitants.* Final report booklets of the sixteen states in this study. Tables No. 1 and No. 9.

51. U. S. Bureau of Census. Census of Population: 1970. *General Population Characteristics.* Final report booklets of the states in this study. Chart — "Population by Race and Residence" — and Table No. 17.

52. *Number of Farms,* Crop Reporting Board, SRS, USDA, January, 1972.

53. *Annual Crop Summary,* Crop Reporting Board, SRS, USDA, January, 1972.

54. *Livestock and Poultry,* Crop Reporting Board, SRS, USDA, January, 1972.

55. U. S. Bureau of the Census. *Census of Manufactures, 1967.*

White and Non-White Population: The classification of the population by color is not ordinarily based on replies to census questions asked by the enumerators but rather is obtained by observation. This concept does not, therefore, reflect a clear-cut definition of biological stock. The non-white population consists of Negroes, American Indians, Japanese, Chinese, Filipinos, and some other groups. Persons of mixed parentage are placed in the color classification of the non-white parent. Persons of Mexican birth or ancestry who are not definitely Indian or of other non-white stock have been classified as white in all censuses except that of 1930. In the 1930 Census, Mexicans were classified as non-white.[1]

1970 Racial Definition: The concept of race as used by the Bureau of the Census in 1970 reflects self-identification by respondents. The 1970 census obtained information on race primarily through self-enumeration, the data represent essentially self-classification by people according to the race with which they identify themselves.

For persons of mixed parentage who were in doubt as to their classification, the race of the person's father was used. In 1960, persons who reported mixed parentage of white and any other race were classified according to the other race; mixtures of races other than white were classified according to the race of the father.

The category "white" includes persons who indicated their race as white, as well as persons who did not classify themselves in one of the specific race categories on the questionnaire but entered Mexican, Puerto Rican, or a response suggesting Indo-European stock.

The category "Negro" includes persons who indicated their race as Negro or Black, as well as persons who did not classify themselves in one of the specific race categories on the questionnaire, but who had such entries as Jamaican, Trinidadian, West Indian, Haitian, and Ethiopian. The term "Negro and other races" includes persons of all races other than white.

Urban/Rural Population: According to the definition adopted for use in the 1960 Census, the urban population comprises all persons living in (a) places of 2,500 inhabitants or more incorporated as cities, boroughs, villages, and towns (except towns in New England, New York and Wisconsin); (b) the densely settled urban fringe, whether incorporated or unincorporated, or urbanized areas; (c) towns in New England and townships in New Jersey and Pennsylvania which contain no incorporated municipalities as subdivisions and have either 25,000 inhabitants or more or a population of 2,500 to 25,000 and a density of 1,500 persons or more to a square mile; (d) counties in states other than the New England States, New Jersey and Pennsylvania that have no incorporated municipalities within their boundaries and have a density of 1,500 persons per square mile; and (e) unincorporated places of 2,500 inhabitants or more. In other words, the urban population comprises all persons living in urbanized areas and in places of 2,500 inhabitants or more outside urbanized areas. The population not classified as urban constitutes the rural population.

Substantially the same definition was used in the 1950 Census, the difference being confined to the urban towns in New England and to urban townships in New Jersey and Pennsylvania. In censuses prior to 1950, the urban population comprise all persons living in incorporated places of 2,500 inhabitants or more and areas (usually minor civil divisions) classified as urban under somewhat different special rules relating to population size and density.[2]

1970 Urban Definition: The 1970 criteria are essentially the same as those used in 1960 with two exceptions. The extended city concept is new for 1970. Secondly, in 1960, towns in the New England States, townships in New Jersey and Pennsylvania, and counties elsewhere, which were classified as urban in accordance with specific criteria, were included in the contiguous urbanized areas. In 1970 only those portions of towns and townships in these States that met

---

1. Bureau of the Census. *Historical Statistics of the United States, Colonial Times to 1957,* pp. 2 and 9.

2. Bureau of the Census. *Census of Population: 1960,* Vol. I Pt. A, p. XII.

the rules followed in defining urbanized areas elsewhere in the United States are included.

Extended cities. — Over the 1960-1970 decade there has been an increasing trend toward the extension of city boundaries to include territory essentially rural in character. Examples are city-county consolidations such as the creation of the city of Chesapeake, Va., from South Norfolk City and Norfolk County and the extension of Oklahoma City, Okla., into five counties. The classification of all the inhabitants of such cities as urban would include in the urban population persons whose environment is primarily rural in character. In order to separate these people from those residing in the closely settled portions of such cities, the Bureau of the Census examined patterns of population density and classified a portion or portions of each such city as rural. An extended city contains one or more areas, each of at least 5 square miles in extent and with a population density of less than 100 persons per square mile according to the 1970 census. The area or areas constitute at least 25 percent of the land area of the legal city or total 25 square miles or more.

These cities—designated as extended cities—thus consist of an urban part and a rural part. When an extended city is a central city of an urbanized area or a standard metropolitan statistical area, only the urban part is considered as the central city. If the extended city is shown separately under the area, the city name is followed by the term "urban part." In tables in which the city name is not followed by this term, the populations figure shown is for the entire city.

Farm: For the 1958 Census of Agriculture, the definition of a farm was based primarily on a combination of "acres in the place" and the estimated value of agriculture sold.

The word "place" was defined to include all land under the control or supervision of one person or partnership at the time of enumeration and on which agricultural operations were conducted at any time in 1959.

Places of 10 or more acres in 1959 were counted as farms if the estimated sale of agricultural products for the year amounted to at least $50. Place of less than 10 acres in 1959 were counted as farms if the estimated sales of agricultural products for the year amounted to at least $250. Places not meeting the minimum estimated level of sales in 1959 were nevertheless counted as farms if they could normally be expected to produce agricultural products in sufficient quantity to meet the requirements of the definition.

In 1950 agricultural operations were defined to include every place of three or more acres, whether or not the operator considered it a farm, and every place having "specialized operations," regardless of the acreage. "Specialized operations" referred to nurseries and greenhouses and to places having 100 or more poultry, production of 300 or more dozen eggs in 1949, or 3 or more hives of bees.

For the 1950 Census of Agriculture, places of 3 or more acres were counted as farms if the annual **value** of agricultural products, whether for home use or for sale but exclusive of home-garden products, amounted to $150 or more. Places of less than 3 acres were counted as farms only if the annual sales of agricultural products amounted to $150 or more. A few places with very low agricultural production because of unusual circumstances, such as crop failures, were also counted as farms if they normally could have been expected to meet the minimum value or sales criteria. The decrease in the number of farms in 1950 and 1959, as compared with earlier censuses, was partly due to changes in the farm definition, especially with respect to places of 3 or more acres in size.

The definition of a census farm has been changed several times since 1850. However in all censuses, the essential features of the farm definition have been that: (1) the land should be under the control of one person and (2) that the land should be used for or connected with agricultural operations.

The requirement that the tracts of land be operated by one person has resulted in the counting of places operated by tenants, sharecroppers, and managers as separate farms. The requirement that all tracts operated by one person be considered one farm resulted in counting as one farm, places comprising owned land and rented land, and tracts of land operated by one person but widely separated as to location.

Agricultural operations have been considered to include the growing of crops; the raising of domestic animals, poultry, and bees; and the production of other agricultural products, including the production of livestock on public lands and open ranges not under the exclusive control of a single individual.

MINIMUM CRITERIA FOR CENSUS FARMS OF 3 OR MORE ACRES:

CENSUSES OF 1850 to 1959[3]

Census year	Minimum value of agricultural products produced for home use or for sale (dollars)	Minimum value of agricultural products sold (dollars)	Other criteria	Reduction in number of farms because of change in definition
1959[1]	Not applied	50	None	232,000
1954	150	Not applied	None	160,000
1950	150	Not applied	None	
1945	150[2]	Not applied	Agricultural operations comprising 3 or more acres of cropland or pastureland	
1940	Not applied	Not applied	Agricultural operations	
1935	Not applied	Not applied	Agricultural operations	
1930	Not applied	Not applied	Agricultural operations	
1925	Not applied	Not applied	Agricultural operations	
1920	Not applied	Not applied	Agricultural operations	
1910	Not applied	Not applied	Agricultural operations	
1900	Not applied	Not applied	Agricultural operations and continuous services of at least 1 person.	
1890	Not applied	Not applied	Agricultural operations	
1880	Not applied	Not applied	Agricultural operations	
1870	Not applied	Not applied	Agricultural operations	
1860	100	Not applied	None	
1850	100	Not applied	None	

[1] The minimum size criteria for 1959 applied to places of 10 or more acres.

[2] Applied only if farm had less than 3 acres of cropland and pasture.

MINIMUM CRITERIA FOR CENSUS FARMS OF LESS THAN 3 ACRES:

CENSUSES OF 1850 to 1959[3]

Census year	Minimum value of agricultural products produced for home use or for sale (dollars)	Minimum value of agricultural products sold (dollars)	Other criteria	Index number of prices received by farmers (1910-1914 = 100)	Number of farms of less than 3 acres
1959	Not applied	250[1]	None	240	79,000
1954	Not applied	150	None	249	100,000
1950	Not applied	150	None	250	77,000
1945	250	Not applied	None	197	99,000
1940	250	Not applied	None	95	36,000
1935	250	Not applied	None	90	36,000
1930	250	Not applied	None	148	43,000
1925	250	Not applied	None	143	15,000
1920	250[2]	Not applied	None	217	20,000
1910	250[2]	Not applied	None	104	18,000
1900	Not applied	Not applied	Constant services of at least 1 person.	NA	41,000
1890	Not applied	500	None	NA	NA
1880	Not applied	500	None	NA	4,000
1870	Not applied	500	None	NA	NA
1860	100	Not applied	None	NA	NA
1850	100	Not applied	None	NA	NA

NA — Not available

[1] The minimum size criteria for 1959 applied to places of less than 10 acres.

[2] Not applicable when farm required services of at least 1 person.

3. Bureau of Census. *Census of Agriculture: 1959,* Vol. II, General Report, Statistics by Subjects, pp. XXVI-XXVII.

Improved Land: This category includes all land regularly tilled or mowed, land in pasture which has been cleared or tilled, land lying fallow, land in gardens, orchards, vineyards, and nurseries, and land occupied by farm buildings. Substantially the same classification of farm land has been employed at different censuses beginning with 1880. However, in 1920 the definition called for the inclusion as improved land of all pasture land which **had been cleared or tilled,** while in 1910 the only pasture land included as improved land was land **pastured and cropped in rotation.** This change in definition resulted in only a very limited change.[4]

Cropland Harvested: This includes land from which crops were harvested; land from which hay (including wild hay) was cut, and land in small fruits, orchards, vineyards, nurseries, and greenhouses. Land from which two or more crops were harvested was to be counted only once.[5]

Figures for cropland harvested relate to the crop years immediately preceding the Census date; other data relate to the Census date: October and November for 1959; April 1 for 1950, 1940 and 1930; January 1 for 1920; April 15 for 1910; June 1 for earlier censuses.[6]

Farm Population: Farm population figures relate to the civilian population living on farms, regardless of occupation or source of incomes. The determination of whether a household is located on a farm has been made largely by the residents themselves. If the respondent in reply to the inquiry, "Is this house a farm (or ranch)?" answers affirmatively, it is, in most cases, classified as a farm dwelling unit and the occupants as part of the farm population. Excluded are the following: persons living on farmland who rent for cash a home and yard only; persons in summer camps, motels, and tourist camps; and persons in institutions on farmland.[7]

Cotton Bales: Bales are running square bales, counting round as half bales (500 pounds gross). Cotton production excludes linters.[8]

Manufacturing Establishments: The Censuses of 1850 to 1920 use the term "manufacturing establishment" to designate factories or plants whose products were valued at $500 or more, but in 1930 and 1940 the minimum limit was $5,000.[9] Beginning with the 1947 manufacturing census, reports were required from all establishments employing one or more persons at any time during the census year. This change in the minimum size limit in 1947 has not appreciably affected the historical comparability of earlier census figures except for data on number of establishments for a few industries.[10]

Capital: The form of the inquiry regarding capital, at all censuses from 1850 to and including 1880, was so vague and general in its character that it cannot be assumed that any true proportion exists between the statistics on this subject as elicited prior to 1890.[11]

The census from 1890 through 1920 contain data on capital which was compiled on the basis of more specific instructions; however its value is limited to comparisons of very general conditions.[12]

At the Census of 1880, the question on capital read: "Capital (real and personal) invested in the business." At the Census of 1890, live capital, i.e., cash on hand, bills receivable, unsettled ledger accounts, raw materials, stock in process of manufacture, finished products on hand, and other sundries, was for the first time included as a separate and distinct item of capital, and the capital invested in realty was divided between land, buildings, and machinery. The form of inquiry in 1890 and 1900 was so similar that comparison may safely be made.[13]

In the Censuses of 1910 through 1920, the instructions for securing data relating to capital were as follows: "The answer should show the total amount of capital, both owned and borrowed, on the last day of the business year reported. All the items of fixed and live capital may be taken at the amounts carried on the books. If land or buildings are rented, that fact should be stated and no value given. If a part of the land or buildings is owned, the remainder being rented,

4. Bureau of Census. *Fourteenth Census of the United States: 1920,* Vol. V, Agriculture, P. 17.
5. Bureau of Census. *Census of Agriculture: 1959,* Vol. II, General Report, Statistics by Subjects, p. 6.
6. *Ibid,* pp. 58-64.
7. Bureau of the Census. *Historical Statistics of the U.S., Colonial Times to 1957,* p. 40.
8. Bureau of the Census. *Census of Agriculture: 1959,* Vol. II, General Report, Statistics by Subjects, pp. 829, 835.

9. Bureau of Census. *Statistical Abstract: 1942,* p. 885.
10. Bureau of Census. *Census of Manufactures: 1963,* Vol. 1, pp. 5-9
11. Bureau of Census. *Twelfth Census of the United States: 1900;* Vol. VIII, Pt. II, p. viii.
12. Bureau of Census. *Fourteenth Census of the United States: 1920,* Vol. IX, p. 17.
13. Bureau of the Census. *Twelfth Census of the United States: 1900,* Vol. VIII, Pt. II, p. viii.

that fact should be so stated and only the value of the owned property given. Do not include securities and loans representing investments in other enterprises."[14] After the Census of 1920, this item was discontinued.

Average Number of Wage Earners: At the censuses of 1850, 1860, and 1870, the inquiries regarding employees called for "average number of hands employed." The inquiries of 1880 were similar. In the Census of 1890 the average number of persons employed during the entire year was called for; and the average number was computed for the actual time the establishments were reported as being in operation. At the census of 1900 the greatest and least numbers of employees were reported, and also the average number employed during each month of the year. The average number of wage earners (men, women and children) employed during the entire year was computed in the Census office by using 12, the number of calendar months, as a divisor into the total of the average numbers reported for each month. This difference in the method of ascertaining the average number of wage-earners during the entire year has resulted in a variation in the average number as between these two censuses, and should be considered in making comparisons.

The schedules for 1890 included in the wage earning class "overseers and foremen or superintendents (not general superintendents or managers)," while the census of 1900 separate from the wage earning class such salaried employees as general superintendents, clerks and salesmen. Therefore this item varies in exactness.[15]

In the census of 1900, persons engaged in manufacturing were shown as (1) Proprietors and firm members (2) Salaried officials, clerks, etc., and (3) Wage earners. In the Census of 1910 the following categories were used: (1) Proprietors and firm members, not including the stockholders of incorporated companies or the members of cooperative associations; (2) Salaried officials of corporations; (3) Superintendents, (4) Managers, clerks, and other salaried employees; (5) Wage earners including pieceworkers. Further inquiry in regard to wage earners called for the number employed on the 15th of each month.[16]

The Census of 1920 continued the foregoing categories of employees except that it included superintendents in one category. As in 1900 and 1910, the average number of wage earners was computed by dividing the sum of the numbers reported for the several months by 12.[17]

The Census of 1930 made a distinction between salaried officers and employees on the one hand, and wage earners on the other. Wage earners were defined as skilled and unskilled workers of all classes, including piece-workers employed at the plant, and foremen and overseers in minor positions who perform work similar to that done by the employees under their supervision. The average was computed in the same manner as previous censuses.[18]

The Census of 1940 defined wage earners as those who perform manual work, using tools, operating machines, handling materials and products, and caring for the plant and its equipment. They comprise both time and piece workers. Working foremen and "gang and straw bosses" are treated as wage earners, but foremen whose duties are primarily supervisory are classified as salaried employees. Averaging was done in the manner used in previous censuses.[19]

Manufacturing: The Census of 1900 and earlier censuses included establishments engaged in the neighborhood, household, and hand industries. The number of establishments canvassed was therefore relatively far greater at these earlier censuses than at the censuses following 1900, but as the establishments in the neighborhood, household, and hand industries are for the most part small, the other criteria show less change. For comparative purposes the statistics for 1899 (but not 1900) have been revised by the Bureau of the Census so as to exclude these neighborhood, household and hand industries. The censuses of 1909 and 1910 and later years were confined to manufacturing establishments conducted under what is known as the factory system, exclusive of the so-called neighborhood, household and hand industries.[20]

Manufacturing is currently defined as the mechanical or chemical transformation of inorganic or organic substances into new products.

14. Bureau of the Census. *Fourteenth Census of the United States: 1920,* Vol. IX, p. 17.
15. Bureau of the Census. *Twelfth Census of the U.S.: 1900,* Vol. VIII, Pt. II, p. viii.
16. *Thirteenth Census of the U.S.: 1910,* Vol. VIII, p. 237.

17. Bureau of Census. *Fourteenth Census of the U.S.: 1920,* Vol. IX, p. 16.
18. Bureau of Census. *Fifteenth Census of the U.S.: 1930,* Manufactures 1929, Vol. I, p. 5.
19. Bureau of Census. *Sixteenth Census of the U.S.: 1940,* Manufactured 1939, Vol. I, p. 4.
20. Bureau of Census. *Thirteenth Census of the U.S.: 1910, Vol. VIII, p. 19.*

The assembly of component parts of products is also considered to be manufacturing if the resulting product is neither a structure nor other fixed improvement. These activities are usually carried on in plants, factories, or mills, which characteristically use power-driven machines and materials-handling equipment.

Manufacturing production is usually carried on for the wholesale market, for transfer to other plants of the same company, or to the order of industrial users rather than for direct sales to the household consumer. However, some manufacturers (e.g., baking, milk bottling, etc.) sell chiefly at retail to household consumers through the mail, through house-to-house routes, or through salesmen. Some activities of a service nature (enameling, binding, plate making, etc.) are included in manufacturing when they are performed primarily for the trade; but they are considered nonmanufacturing when they are performed primarily to the order of the household consumer. On the other hand, some manufacturing industries include business firms which do not undertake physical production but perform only the entrepreneural function of buying the materials, designing, and marketing the product, and have the actual production done on contract (e.g., apparel jobbers).

Other related and diverse supporting activities are likewise included in the definition of manufacturing and are described in greater detail in the current Bureau of Census reports.[21]

General Statistics for Manufacturing Establishments

Establishments: The Census of Manufactures is conducted on an establishment basis. That is, a company operating establishments at more than one location is required to submit a report for each location; also a company engaged in distinctly different lines of activity at one location is required to submit separate reports if the plan records permit such a separation and if the activities are substantial in size.

Census tabulations of establishment reports, therefore, differ substantially from those prepared on a company basis, i.e., from consolidated reports which combine various types of activities at different locations (thereby yielding a net sales figure for the industry exclusive of interplant transfers but making meaningful geographic tabulations of employment and value added impossible). These consolidated reports also include nonmanufacturing activities of companies primarily engaged in manufacturing.

From 1947 through 1963 reports from manufacturing establishments have been required from all establishments employing one or more persons at any time during the census year.

In the 1939 and earlier censuses, establishments with less than $5,000 value of products were excluded. The change in the minimum size limit in 1947 has not appreciably affected the historical comparability of earlier census figures except for data on number of establishments for a few industries.[22]

All Employees: The category "all employees" comprises all full-time and part-time employees on the payrolls of operating manufacturing establishments who worked or received pay for any part of the pay period which included the 12th and ended nearest the 15th of the months specified on the report forms. At the all-industry level, the employees of central administrative offices and auxiliaries are included. Included are all persons on paid sick leave, paid holidays, and paid vacations during these pay periods. Excluded are members of the Armed Forces and pensioners carried on the active rolls but not working during the period. Officers of corporations are included as employees; proprietors and partners of unincorporated firms, however, are excluded from the total.

Employment and payroll total for central administrative offices and auxiliaries are included in the statistics shown for the years 1954 to 1963. Prior to 1954, this information was not available. The "number of establishments with 20 or more employees" total for 1958 and all previous years and "total number of establishments" total for 1954 and previous years does not include data for central administrative offices and auxiliaries.[23]

Production and Related Workers: This category comprises workers (up through the working foreman level) engaged in fabricating, processing, assembling, inspection, receiving, storage, handling, packing, warehousing, shipping (but not delivering) maintenance, repair,

21. Bureau of Census. *Census of Manufactures: 1963,* Vol. 1, pp. 5-9

22. Bureau of Census. *Census of Manufactures: 1963,* Vol. 1, Summary and Subject Statistics, p. 7.

23. Bureau of Census. *Census of Manufactures: 1963,* Vol. 1, Summary Subject Statistics pp. 16, 102.

janitorial, watchman services, product development, auxiliary production for plant's own use (e.g., power plant), record keeping, and other services closely associated with these production operations at the establishment covered by the report. Supervisory employees above the working foreman level are excluded from this category.[24]

Man-hours: This total consists of all plant man-hours of production and related workers as defined above. It represents all man-hours worked or paid for at the plant including actual overtime hours (not straight-time equivalent hours). It excludes hours paid for vacations, holidays, or sick-leave, when the employee was not at the plant. Where employees elected to work during the vacation period, only actual hours worked by such employees were reported.

Man-hours were generally well reported except in some industries, such as apparel, where work is commonly performed on a piece-rate basis. However, man-hours were not collected for the very small establishments. Man-hours were estimated for these small establishments as well as for other non-reporters. Because estimating was largely confined to small establishments, there is no significant qualification to the validity of overall geographic area totals for man-hours, except for sawmills and a few other industries characterized by small establishments.[25]

Value added by manufacture, adjusted: Value added by manufacture is derived by subtracting the total cost of materials (including materials, supplies, fuel, electric energy, cost of resales and miscellaneous receipts) from the value of shipments (including resales) and other receipts and adjusting the resulting amount by the net change in finished products and work-in-process inventories between the beginning and end of the year.[26]

Capital Expenditures: This category includes expenditures made during the year for permanent additions and major alterations to plants as well as new machinery and equipment purchases, that were chargeable to fixed asset accounts of manufacturing establishments and were of a type for which depreciation accounts are ordinarily maintained. Expenditures for machinery and equipment include those made for replacement purposes, as well as for additions to plant capacity. Excluded from such expenditure total are costs of maintenance and repairs charged as current operating expense; new facilities and equipment leased from non-manufacturing concerns; new facilities owned by the Federal Government but operated under contract by private companies; and plant and equipment furnished to the manufacturer by communities and organization.

For the years of 1958 to 1963, "capital expenditures" includes expenditures for plants under construction but not in operation in addition to expenditures at operating manufacturing establishments. Prior to 1958, the data represents expenditures at operating manufacturing establishments only.[27]

Dates of Censuses

Population:

	1970	April 1
	1960	April 1
	1950-1930	April 1
	1920	January 1
	1910	April 15
	1830-1900	June 1
	1790-1820	1st Monday in August[28]

Agriculture:

	1959	October 7, 1959-Nov. 18, 1959
	1930-50	April 1
	1920	January 1
	1910	April 15
	1840-1900	June 1[29]

24. *Ibid.* p. 16.
25. *Ibid.* p. 17.
26. *Ibid*, p. 22.

27. Bureau of Census. *Census of Manufactures: 1963*, Vol. I, Summary and Subject Statistics, p. 102.
28. Bureau of Census. *Census of Population: 1960,* Vol. 1, pt. A, p. VI.
29. Bureau of Census. *Census of Agriculture: 1959, p.*